MW00650320

World Scientific Book Series in Marketing

Series Editor: Chezy Ofir
(The Hebrew University of Jerusalem, Israel)

Published:

Vol. 1:   *Finding Wisdom in Brand Tragedies: Managing Threats to*
            Brand Equity
            by Robert J Thomas

World Scientific Book Series in Marketing

Finding Wisdom in Brand Tragedies

Managing Threats to Brand Equity

World Scientific Book Series in Marketing

Series Editor
Chezy Ofir
Hebrew University of Jerusalem, Israel

Finding Wisdom in Brand Tragedies

Managing Threats to Brand Equity

Robert J Thomas
Georgetown University, USA

World Scientific

NEW JERSEY · LONDON · SINGAPORE · BEIJING · SHANGHAI · HONG KONG · TAIPEI · CHENNAI · TOKYO

Published by

World Scientific Publishing Co. Pte. Ltd.

5 Toh Tuck Link, Singapore 596224

USA office: 27 Warren Street, Suite 401-402, Hackensack, NJ 07601

UK office: 57 Shelton Street, Covent Garden, London WC2H 9HE

Library of Congress Cataloging-in-Publication Data

Names: Thomas, Robert J., 1944–   author.

Title: Finding wisdom in brand tragedies : managing threats to brand equity /
    Robert J Thomas, Georgetown University, USA.

Description: New Jersey : World Scientific, [2023] | Series: World scientific book series in
    marketing ; vol. 1 | Includes bibliographical references.

Identifiers: LCCN 2023006357 | ISBN 9789811268175 (hardcover) |
    ISBN 9789811268182 (ebook for institutions) | ISBN 9789811268199 (ebook for individuals)

Subjects: LCSH: Branding (Marketing) | Business failures.

Classification: LCC HF5415.1255 .T53 2023 | DDC 658.8/27--dc23/eng/20230421

LC record available at https://lccn.loc.gov/2023006357

British Library Cataloguing-in-Publication Data

A catalogue record for this book is available from the British Library.

For any available supplementary material, please visit
https://www.worldscientific.com/worldscibooks/10.1142/13196#t=suppl

Desk Editors: Logeshwaran Arumugam/Sandhya Venkatesh

Typeset by Stallion Press
Email: enquiries@stallionpress.com

For Virginia with All My Love

Preface

What can be learned from seemingly successful brands that ran into very challenging situations threatening their survival? Attempting to answer this question and to better understand why some of those brands disappeared while others survived led me to write this book. Here's how it started. In January 2007, Steve Jobs, the CEO of Apple, showed off his company's new iPhone. His presentation was exciting and motivating, but this announcement was never going to take me away from my trusted Blackberry phone!

Even four years after the iPhone was on the market, the Blackberry was still my phone of choice. However, over time I noticed several of my colleagues had purchased the new Apple iPhone. My questions for them poured forth: "Did the glass keyboard really work? How was the quality? Can I try it? What were the apps like? Was it easy to send and receive calls?" The responses were mostly favorable. Nevertheless, I remained convinced that the Blackberry was the best phone on the market. I could not imagine typing a message without my reliable thumb-driven keyboard.

Unfortunately, all that changed in October 2011. The whole Blackberry system crashed in major parts of the world and in the United States for almost four days during a busy work week. No one had access to the system. For me, this failure created such serious doubts about the future of Blackberry phones that it finally drove me to purchase an Apple iPhone. I wasn't the only one. The results were eventually severe for the Blackberry phone. During 2011, the stock price of Blackberry dropped from $58 to $15. Ultimately, in 2022, Blackberry "decommissioned the infrastructure and services" that supported its phone.

Ironically, while the original Blackberry phone and system were no longer in service, the brand was so strong that the company continued to use it for security products and services for business customers. For me, the loss of my Blackberry phone was a *tragedy*. A tragedy not only for users of the product but also for employees and investors in the firm. Borrowing from the classic meaning of the word, a *tragedy* involves sorrowful events experienced and/or caused by one or more "heroic" individuals. This implies that the source of the tragedy, which can begin outside of a brand and the organization that provides it, can also be caused by one or more individuals involved in leading and managing the brand from within the organization. I wanted to learn more about how and why Blackberry and other firms like it experienced and coped with such a tragedy.

Thus began my exploration to better understand brand tragedies, what's behind them, and the wisdom gained from studying them. The research approach used to develop an understanding of a selection of brand tragedies involved published information derived from a variety of secondary sources. Using this approach to accumulate knowledge about a brand's historical journey in a tragedy facilitates the development of sufficient wisdom about a brand to enable avoiding future tragedies and to take remedial actions to the extent possible when one occurs.

Robert J. Thomas
Washington, DC

About the Author

Robert J. Thomas is Emeritus Professor of Marketing at Georgetown University where he has held numerous leadership positions, launched several new programs, and taught a diverse set of advanced courses in marketing. He received his PhD in marketing from the Wharton School at the University of Pennsylvania and is a Distinguished Research Fellow at the Institute for the Study of Business Markets (ISBM). His publications are in the areas of new product development, market segmentation, organizational buying behavior, business-to-business marketing, and forecasting. His book, *New Product Development: Managing and Forecasting for Strategic Success*, was a featured selection of the Fortune Book Club, and his book *New Product Success Stories: Lessons From Leading Innovators* has been published in several languages. In addition to designing and teaching numerous executive education seminars and workshops in the U.S., Europe, and Asia, he has consulted with over 60 organizations in a wide variety of industries and cultures, including products and services in consumer and business-to-business markets.

Acknowledgments

First and foremost, I would like to acknowledge the contributions of my five Georgetown MBA research assistants whose work supported five chapters in this book. They include Daniella Arias, Chen Chen, Sarah Reid Fletcher, Katherine Miyamasu, and Morgan Swedberg Seymour. Their diligence, intelligence, and competence were important and inspirational to me in completing this book. The contribution of each one is noted in their respective chapters. In addition, I would like to thank James Bubnick, a former Georgetown MBA student, who reviewed selected material in the book from his perspective as a trained engineer.

I would also like to thank Kai Voss, a true brand "Meister," who contributed many years of brand research and thinking that helped build NIVEA into a world class brand. Our work and conversations over the years have motivated me to focus on the brand as the most important driver of business success.

Everyone needs a great role model and advisor like Jerry (Yoram) Wind. As his doctoral student at the Wharton School, I learned a great deal about the link between academic research and practice. More importantly, our collaboration on several papers and his unending contributions to the thought and practice of business continuously encourage and enlighten me.

In many ways, this book would not have been possible without the consistent support and passionate work ethic from Professor Chezy Ofir at the Hebrew University of Jerusalem. I truly benefitted from his world class scholarship and admire his unrelenting drive to add value to the world of marketing thought.

In the process of writing a book, it is essential to have several sparring partners with whom to bounce ideas. For this, I have benefitted tremendously from the strategic and thoughtful insights of Michael Chin and Christina Nunez. In addition, I am especially grateful to my extended family Lisa, Chloe, Lily, and Griffin for their wonderfully creative contributions. Thank you all!

Finally, I would be remiss if I did not thank the wonderful editorial team at World Scientific Publishing Company, including Sandhya, Logesh, and Nandha! Their talent, promptness, responsiveness, and commitment to this book have been extraordinarily helpful.

Contents

Chapter 1

Signposts for Brand Tragedies

A leader of any organization does not want to experience a tragedy that could damage its brand and possibly cripple its business. Yet tragedies to brands can and do happen. Blackberry, Toys "R" Us, Kodak, Blockbuster, Compaq, Pets.com, Radio Shack, Esprit, Living Social, Tylenol, and Peloton are a few of the many brands that have faced tragedies of one kind or another, thereby putting their brands and businesses at risk. Several of these tragedies occurred during the 20th century and new ones emerged in the 21st. While some tragedies may be associated with poor leadership or dysfunctional products and services, a variety of other factors can lead to a brand's demise, including catastrophes or viral disease, such as the COVID-19 pandemic in 2020.

The objective of this book is to find *wisdom* from studying *brand tragedies* to help develop *signposts* that can be used to monitor a brand's well-being. Signposts are essentially constructs that communicate a message to a viewer to anticipate and realize that something relevant is ahead. It is typically used as a signal to prepare for action that helps maintain or change one's course or direction. In simplest terms, it summarizes accumulated practical *wisdom* based on a body of knowledge, principles, and experience that can influence judgment for important decisions. These signposts may or may not prevent a brand tragedy but knowing them will enable leaders to better prepare for and manage one should it occur.

Understanding the meaning of a brand tragedy begins with a basic understanding of how a *tragedy* is viewed throughout this book. A common dictionary definition of a tragedy is a disastrous event,[1] which is often associated with calamitous outcomes, such as natural disasters, wars, crimes, plagues, pandemics, or famines. However, a deeper look into the meaning of a tragedy goes into the "branch of drama that treats in a serious and dignified style the sorrowful or terrible events encountered or caused by a heroic individual."[2] This implies that the source of the tragedy, which can begin outside a brand and the organization that provides it, can also be caused by one or more individuals involved in leading and managing the brand from within the organization.

In the context of a successful brand that may encounter extreme challenges, whatever the source, the "heroic" individuals or management team responsible for the brand — the *brand providers* — must recognize and respond to the challenges. Not doing so or responding poorly can perpetuate a tragedy leading to a brand's decline or in some cases, death. In situations where a brand has experienced a difficult event, the identification and understanding of the "tragic flaw" in the situation and of those involved expose a different kind of learning than the tragedy itself. The purpose of studying the account of a brand's tragedy is not to find fault with its leadership or any specific manager involved but to reveal the tragic flaw and place it in the constellation of flaws from other brand tragedies as a basis for learning and wisdom.

As it often turns out, there are cases when one person is responsible for managing the tragedy, but more frequently, it's a management team. Providing a more nuanced study of notable brand tragedies and how leaders managed them can be a basis for learning how to help prevent or ameliorate the occurrence of future tragedies. Because some brand tragedies can be sudden and some can fester over time, knowing and understanding what leads to brand tragedies in general can better prepare a management team to drive an effective remediation for the brand. Occasionally, a brand provider may inevitably realize that a brand is in such bad condition with customers and other stakeholders that it cannot be revived and is intentionally destroyed. As they say in card games, knowing when to hold and when to fold may preempt future losses.

The Value of Learning from Brand Histories

While so-called "brand tragedies" may appear to be about commercial activities, it has become clear that brands exist on a stage well beyond any profit or non-profit enterprise. Brands can live across generations of customers and transcend the people and organizations that may have created them. Commercial brands can, and have, become part of the social and cultural fabric of many countries. Coca-Cola became such a brand. It was created in 1886 as a carbonated beverage and is recognized in most countries of the world. It carries a consistent core meaning through messages about taste, refreshment, and the positive aspects of life. For example, "Taste the Feeling" was one of its slogans. The products, slogans, ad messages, and promotions changed over the years, but the core meaning of the brand has been consistent.

This embeddedness of the core meaning of the brand was made obvious to the firm in 1985 when its managers launched New Coke as a replacement for the original Coca-Cola beverage. The product reformulation and a new name developed in response to an aggressive competitor (Pepsi Cola) created a strong backlash from those customers who wanted their "real" Coca-Cola.[3] Managers did not expect such a swift and deep response from its customers. Three months later, they reverted back to the original formula! Coca-Cola had become part of the social fabric of everyday life for many people, and changing it was an egregious disruption.

While a complete Coca-Cola brand tragedy was averted, the historical events leading up to it should be studied and questioned. What motivated a group of well-meaning managers to decide to replace the company's core branded cola product just as it was about to celebrate its 100th anniversary? Were they driven by competitive factors, financial considerations, retail relationships, biases, hubris, or other traditional business factors? Any or all of these may help understand the potential New Coke tragedy in this situation (to be considered in greater detail in Chapter 3).

It is in this respect that the aim of this book is to identify and explore the kinds of factors that emerge from studying specific brand tragedies. While these tragedies may be familiar to some and dismissed as poor management or due to some other unfortunate event, a deeper dive into the root causes from an historical perspective can provide uncommon insights. Whether derived from a self-created tragedy or one imposed by external crises, such as a natural catastrophe, understanding how an organization's leadership team and managers identify and respond to a potential tragedy can provide important signposts that are critical to a brand's future.

In this introductory chapter, several factors about brands are considered. First, the definition of a brand and branding provides an understanding of their relevance to business and society. Second, a brief review of the history of brands and branding offers a perspective on their increasing importance, especially for business success. Third, an understanding of the brand in its ecosystem highlights the scope of a brand, especially as sources of signposts for possible tragedies ahead. Fourth, an overview of how brands are traditionally managed delivers a basis for understanding the areas where situations may go right or wrong for a brand. Finally, a brief overview of the remaining chapters is provided as a roadmap to better understand the wisdom that can be garnered from studying brand tragedies and their signposts.

Defining a Brand and Branding

To understand how and why brands have tragedies, it is essential to understand the meaning of a brand and branding. *In its most fundamental form, a brand is a type of data, often expressed as alphanumeric text or images assigned to something (or someone) that meets one or more human needs, with the potential to communicate a meaningful message from a sender to a receiver.* As six letters of text, Google means nothing (although it is reportedly a misspelling of googol, a very large number). When the six letters of text, "Google," are associated with a meaning that is communicated by its sender, such as rapid accessibility to vast amounts of searchable online information to meet one's needs, it becomes a "brand" with the potential to mean far more to those who receive the message than the six letters. It follows that *branding* is the process of assigning the "brand" to something (or someone) that meets one or more human needs.

Branding began when humans named people, animals, and things for basic needs, such as recognition, identification, communication, or differentiation. Like people, brands are born; they can grow, mature, and die. Unlike people, brands can live for extended lengths of time, even hundreds or thousands of years. For example, many great writers and artists have passed away, but their work, branded by their names, lives on. Austen, Da Vinci, Dickinson, Durer, Gibran, Hemingway, Joyce, Michelangelo, O'Keefe, Picasso, Rembrandt, Shakespeare, and others illustrate the longevity of these "brands."

Not surprisingly, the usage of brands and brand building has become very common and purposeful, especially in the practice of marketing. The growing focus on brands is well documented in Christine Moorman's annual Chief Marketing Officer (CMO) studies. In 2021, she reported that planned marketing spending on *brand building* was reported as 9.3% of marketing budgets, second only to new product introductions at 10.1%.[4]

People and organizations that offered products and services for sale eventually began to recognize the potential value of creative branding. Brands travel beyond borders, from local to national to global entities. Companies such as Apple, Chanel, Coca-Cola, Disney, GE, Google, Meta (Facebook), McDonald's, Mercedes, Microsoft, Nike, NIVEA, Samsung, and 3M have become widely recognized brands in many parts of the world. Each carries a certain meaning with its name that enables current and potential customers to recognize them, differentiate them from others, experience them, communicate about them, and in a commercial context, purchase and use them to meet needs, thereby creating value for the brand provider and user.

Consider the cartoon character brand Mickey Mouse, created by Walt Disney in 1928. Mickey Mouse epitomizes how a brand can reach iconic status at multiple levels in the minds of children and adults in many countries.[5] On a commercial level, the Walt Disney Company, its employees, investors, and other stakeholders benefit financially from Mickey Mouse films, cartoons, television shows, comic books, theme parks, toys, and other merchandise. On a customer level, adults trust that their children will be safe and in good hands watching and being entertained by a Mickey Mouse cartoon or using other Mickey Mouse products.

On a social and cultural level, Mickey Mouse has been the subject of art by Andy Warhol, Claes Oldenburg, and Roy Lichtenstein, thereby transcending the commercial aspects of the brand into the history of modern art. In effect, a brand can also be construed as a "commons" or a resource in which multiple stakeholders have access to it and an interest in its existence — including the brand creators, customers, and social and cultural institutions. In this sense, it is also possible that a brand has the potential to become a "tragedy of the commons" if individuals or groups who have access to it use their self-interest to diminish or spoil the brand in some way. As noted by Nitin Rakesh and Jerry Wind, when brands become vulnerable to poor management decisions, fake information, and other challenges, it results in the loss of confidence in brands.[6]

A Brief History of Brands

According to the University of Texas at Austin Linguistics Research Center, the word *brand* apparently derived from the Old Norse word *brandr*, which translates into English as a "piece of firewood."[7] While the

Old Norse language and versions of it date back to the period between the seventh and fifteenth centuries,[8] the concept and action of commercial branding arose much earlier during the Early Bronze IV age from about 2250–2000 BCE in the Indus Valley.[9] Merchants employed the practice of putting seals on their pottery and other wares to identify the maker. As noted by Stanley Wolpert[10]:

> These magnificent seals, probably made for merchants who used them to "brand" their wares, provide brilliant portraits of Brahmani bulls, 'unicorns,' tigers, and other animals, whose realistic likenesses reappear two thousand years later on the capital plinths of the pillars of Ashoka.

Figure 1.1 shows an example of how early Egyptians branded their livestock. This apparently created sufficient value for other merchants and farmers that branding became a common process through the centuries.

The development of the printing press by Johannes Gutenberg in the mid-1400s AD gave rise to the use of brands in print. As an example, around 1494–1495, Aldus Manutius founded the Aldine Press in Venice and by 1500 began to use the image of an anchor draped by a dolphin to

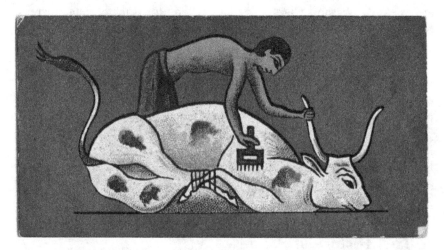

Figure 1.1.   Ancient Egypt [Branding the Cattle]

Source: George Arents Collection, The New York Public Library. "Ancient Egypt. [Branding the cattle]." New York Public Library Digital Collections. Accessed September 20, 2020. http://digitalcollections.nypl.org/items/510d47da-98af-a3d9-e040-e00a18064a99.

Figure 1.2.   Symbolic Brand Logo Adopted by Aldus Manutius, Circa. 1500

Source: Wikimedia Commons, the free media repository, https://commons.wikimedia.org/wiki/File:Aldus-symbol.jpg. (Accessed February 24, 2023).

identify or brand his press (see Figure 1.2). The symbol, derived from an old Roman coin, was associated with the Latin phrase "Festina lente," translating to "make haste slowly."[11] Thus, Manutius not only developed one of the first commercial applications of a brand to identify his publishing operation but he also developed a slogan or early form of a *positioning* statement, both of which are established marketing tools today.

Not long after the development of printing to reproduce books, artists began the practice of establishing symbols or logos to identify and promote their art. One of the most successful and celebrated artists of his time was Albrecht Dürer (1471–1528). Dürer was known widely for his

Figure 1.3.   Self-portrait, Albrecht Durer, 1500 (note iconic monogram or brand in upper left part of the portrait)

Source: Wikimedia Commons contributors, "File: Albrecht Dürer — 1500 self-portrait (High resolution and detail).jpg," Wikimedia Commons, the free media repository, https://commons.wikimedia.org/w/index.php?title=File:Albrecht_D%C3%BCrer_-_1500_self-portrait_(High_resolution_and_detail).jpg&oldid=450783551 (Accessed August 16, 2022).

engravings, paintings, and printmaking. His most iconic work, a self-portrait dated 1500 (Figure 1.3), notably displays a stylized monogram in the upper left half of the painting that became his logo or what would be called his trademark to identify his *brand*. Dürer's popularity was so strong that patrons would purchase a painting or print based solely on the artist's logo.

Unfortunately, Dürer's popularity encouraged forgery of his work. In 1506, Dürer brought what is considered to be the first art forgery case to the court in Venice.[12] This intellectual property lawsuit was placed against another artist and a printer who copied his painting *Christ Among the Doctors in the Temple*. The Venice court agreed with Dürer and instructed the forgers to remove Dürer's logo from their reproductions; however, they were allowed to continue selling the copies as "after Dürer." Unfortunately, the illegal copying of successful brands continues to be a problem for many firms, organizations, and individuals. Nevertheless, this set the stage for many artists, poets, writers, and other artisans to differentiate and value their work with a branded identity.

It did not take long for business firms to see the value in purposively creating and commercializing brands with names, even against the risk of copies. It has been reported that in the early 16th century, the Scots branded wooden casks of whiskey with the name of the producer burned on top of each barrel.[13] This was reportedly done to identify and protect the distillers from copiers so that customers knew they were getting the brand they wanted from the taverns they visited. The Belgian brewery, Den Hoorn, founded in 1366 became the home of the Stella Artois brand in 1708 when the brewery was purchased by Sebastian Artois — a brand that still enjoys success in the 21st century.[14]

In 1670, King Charles II of England signed a charter creating the Hudson's Bay Company for purposes of fur trading, a brand that still exists despite struggling with the COVID-19 crisis.[15] In 1752, Caswell-Massey was founded in Newport, Rhode Island, as an apothecary and perfumery, a brand still enjoying success as one of the oldest sources of personal care products in the United States.[16] As the functionality and value of brands became evident, how best to create, care for, commercialize, and understand the ecosystem in which they lived became a business imperative.

The Brand and its Ecosystem

A brand does not exist alone. As shown in Figure 1.4, it is part of an ecosystem with various stakeholders, all of whom may have an interest in the brand in some form or another. Any tragedy that affects a brand also has a potential impact on its stakeholders. The origin of a brand typically begins with the *brand provider*, the primary stakeholder. It is the firm or organization that originates and takes responsibility for the brand. Developing and bringing a brand to life may require a variety of suppliers, who deliver components, ingredients, packaging, communication, expertise, and other inputs to the firm. Delivering the brand may involve a

Figure 1.4.   Illustration of Brand Stakeholder Ecosystem

number of channel partners, including wholesalers, retailers, media, regulators, and other social institutions. Experiencing the brand are customers who may be individuals, families, or organizations.

The term "customer" and "consumer" are often used interchangeably. The more inclusive term "customer" will be used throughout this book. It is an umbrella term that can be a person, organization, social unit (e.g., family), or artificially intelligent machine (e.g., automated order replenishment). It is a term that also includes multiple roles in the brand purchase and experience process: those who influence the purchase of a brand, those who decide to purchase it, those who purchase it, those who use it, and/or those who talk about it with others. The term "consumer" often refers to the "ultimate user" of the brand, which can sometimes be a narrow interpretation.

To better comprehend and even avoid tragedies, the brand provider must manage an understanding of the brand among the stakeholders illustrated in Figure 1.4 to gain their support and cooperation, especially when needed. The history, quality, vitality, and continuity of the brand among these stakeholders must be understood and managed. This has become more important as the speed of communication between and among stakeholders has rapidly accelerated in the 21st century. The Internet, social media, and related technologies have facilitated greater opportunities for digital connectivity among people to talk about brands, including their benefits, problems, and sometimes tragedies.

The volume and velocity with which digital information occurs can impact a brand well before any damage is fully understood. Consider the impact of the video taken of a United Airlines passenger removed from his seat and dragged down the aisle of the plane by airline security agents prior to takeoff. The video went viral on social media almost immediately and set the stage for a brand tragedy. The news emerged in traditional and social media nationwide. How do customers respond, how does it influence a brand's value, and how do firms recover? When brand relationships between an organization and its customers are at risk, it becomes imperative for an organization's leadership and management to assess the situation and take some form of remedial action.

The Strategic Management of Brands

While brands and branding became well established in the commercial arena in the early 20th century, business firms became very serious about managing them after the 1981 publication of the book *Positioning* by Al Ries and Jack Trout.[17] Their view of positioning was about how the name of a product, person, organization, or other entity was perceived by customers, whether business-to-business (B2B) or business-to-consumer (B2C). A company can create a brand but then has to build its position in the mind of customers to realize beneficial outcomes.

For Ries and Trout, the name of the brand was a critical decision. Ideally, if a brand carried existing meaning, it opened the door into what was already present in the customer's mind. They used the example of the DieHard automotive battery brand marketed by Sears Holdings. In this case, the name links to a key benefit associated with a battery: that it is long lasting and durable — it will not die easily. So, a brand's positioning is not as much about the product as it is about the core need met by it. That does not say the product, its price, nor its availability is unimportant; it just indicates that the brand name enables a communication pathway or connection to a customer's mind which expeditiously reinforces its meaning and value to the customer. It also does not say that a brand with no prior meaning in the customer's mind can't be built; it is possible but will most likely take substantial communication to do so.

While a brand's name and its positioning are important starting points, it is critical to understand why branding has become and remains a central activity among profit and non-profit organizations. A major reason is the emergence of the concept of *brand equity*, which has been defined by David Aaker as "a set of brand assets and liabilities linked to a brand, its name and symbol, that add to or subtract from the value provided by a product or service to a firm and/or to that firm's customers."[18] Anything that is so visible and that can add or subtract value, financial or otherwise, becomes a source of opportunity and competitive advantage for any organization seeking to improve its performance but also opens the door for potential tragedy. Part of the motivation of this book is that the majority of thinking about brands is on the "assets" part of the brand equity equation, often ignoring the "liability" aspects. The focus on brand tragedies recognizes liability factors that can challenge the value of a brand — hence the sub-title of this book: Managing Threats to Brand Equity.

A consequence of the importance and complexity of branding has been an increased focus on properly developing and managing the brand. There are numerous textbooks and popular books on the topic of brands and "strategic brand management," each with a somewhat different approach. For example, one text considers the sociocultural meaning of brands, brand equity, brand building, and managing brands.[19] Another textbook provides a four-component model of strategic brand management: building brands, leveraging brands, identifying and measuring brands, and protecting brands.[20]

Another text takes a deep and provocative look at brand management focusing on understanding brands, brand management, and brand evaluation.[21] Yet another leading text proposes a four-step process to strategically manage brands: (1) identifying and developing brand plans, (2) designing and implementing brand marketing programs, (3) measuring and interpreting brand performance, and (4) growing and sustaining brand equity.[22] Each of their steps contains numerous key concepts for a total of some 16 concepts that facilitate the management of a brand.

The underpinning for most of these various views of strategic brand management is a core marketing framework that is comprised of knowing the factors that influence a market, segmenting your market for advantage, positioning your brand in the segment, and developing and implementing a marketing plan that includes the so-called 4Ps of marketing: the **product** offering and all its benefits to customers, the **price** and its associated value, the **place** where the product offering is available, and the **promotion** or marketing communication that establishes the brand's positioning among selected customers.

While this framework may be considered the core of a strategic marketing process, in practice, there is considerable interaction among the parts of the framework for it to be successful in supporting a brand with customers. How a firm defines and embraces the marketing framework and puts it into practice as an integrated process has an important influence on a firm's performance. A deeper review of these core aspects of marketing management can be found in more traditional marketing textbooks.[23]

Summary and Structure of the Book

Brands and branding have deep historical roots. Almost anything or anyone can be branded with a name or mark for commercial or other purposes. As Grant Reid, President and CEO of Mars, Inc., makers of food products (including brands such as Snickers and M&M's), has been quoted: "We're basically an agricultural company that takes ingredients, from corn to cocoa, and turns them into brands. That's really what we do."[24] The act of branding initiates activities in a brand ecosystem among people and organizations who have a vested interest in the brand and who may receive value from it.

Occasionally, a brand will experience a tragedy that can put its value and equity at risk. Pundits will often conclude there is a primary reason for a specific brand's tragedy, and in some situations, that is the case. However, in other situations, studying them more deeply can reveal tragic flaws in the actions of key decision makers in response to brand-challenging experiences. Examining the backstories of a selection of relatively well-known brands that have experienced tragedy can inform how and why some survived and some did not. Doing so may help leaders and managers of current brands avoid the miscues that lead to brand tragedies.

Perhaps more importantly, for those brands that have survived — or even thrived — after a tragedy, how did they do it? How did Chipotle, the Mexican food restaurant chain, which suffered debilitating setbacks with food-borne illnesses among its patrons, fight back to rebuild its business? How did United Airlines respond to its crisis after a passenger was dragged off one of its flights? Studying various tragedies and identifying signposts that can inform thinking and decision-making may help anticipate a potential tragedy and possibly revive a brand when tragedy strikes. The book considers six different yet somewhat related signposts that can signal trouble ahead for a brand.

The signposts include *technology myopia*, *ruptured loyalties*, *bruising viral spirals*, *catastrophes*, *leadership lost*, and *psychic prisons*. Ironically, there is very little systematic logic to structure these signposts into some kind of business process. All involve some forms of activities from both internal and external sources. Furthermore, all are different in their sources and consequences, and some are interactive. For example, *technology myopia* among the managers of an organization can be a contributor to organization finding itself in a *psychic prison*, unable to respond effectively to crises brought on by new technologies.

Importantly, this is not a "how to" book, although there are selected tools that can help better manage brand tragedies. In Chapter 8, a Brand Tragedy Index is proposed based on the six signposts considered in Chapters 2–7. The index is defined by *propositions* emerging from each of the six different tragedies. By framing the propositions as vulnerabilities to selected factors defining the tragedy, an indicator to the potential occurrence of one is provided. All brands are susceptible to tragedies, yet astute leaders will anticipate potential problems if they can recognize the *signposts* that indicate trouble ahead and possibly prepare for, resolve, or turn such issues into opportunities.

In summary, the book is about discovering and understanding that brands play an important role in the lives of customers and other stakeholders in its ecosystem. It is a book for current and future leaders and managers who need to understand the vital importance of a brand for organizational success. It is for those who want to build and manage their brands to maintain and continuously improve their value for customers, employees, shareholders, and the well-being of society. While there will be no one right approach or silver bullet to avert or ameliorate a specific tragedy, the better-prepared leaders and managers are for a brand tragedy, the greater the likelihood of an expedient and constructive outcome when one occurs.

Endnotes

1. Merriam-Webster.com Dictionary, s.v. "Tragedy," https://www.merriam-webster.com/dictionary/tragedy (Accessed February 22, 2022).
2. Sewall, Richard B. and Leonard W. Conversi, "Tragedy," *Encyclopedia Britannica,* December 20, 2021, https://www.britannica.com/art/tragedy-literature. See also Osborne, Harold, "The Concept of Tragedy," *The British Journal of Aesthetics,* 15(4), April 1975, 287–293.
3. Allen, Frederick, *Secret Formula.* New York: Open Road Integrated Media, 2015.
4. Moorman, Christine, "The CMO Survey: Managing and Measuring Marketing Spending for Growth and Returns," 2021, https://cmosurvey.org/wp-content/uploads/2021/08/The_CMO_Survey-Highlights_and_Insights_Report-August_2021.pdf.
5. Apgar, Garry, *Mickey Mouse: Emblem of the American Spirit.* San Francisco, CA: Weldon Owen, 2015. See also, Coleman, Barbara, "Through the Years We'll All Be Friends: The 'Mickey Mouse Club,' Consumerism, and the Cultural Consensus," *Visual Resources,* 14(3), 1999, 297–306.
6. Rakesh, Nitin and Jerry Wind, *Transformation in Times of Crisis.* Chennai, Tamil Nadu, India: Notion Press, 2020.
7. University of Texas at Austin, Linguistics Research Center, https://lrc.la.utexas.edu/eieol_base_form_dictionary/norol/18 (Accessed February, 2022).
8. König, Ekkehard and Johan van der Auwera, eds., *The Germanic Languages.* London: Routledge, 1994.
9. Moore, Karl and Reid, Susan, "The Birth of Brand: 4000 Years of Branding History," *Business History,* 4(50), July 2008, 419–432.
10. Wolpert, Stanley, *A New History of India,* 8th ed. New York: Oxford University Press, 2009, p. 16.
11. Fletcher, George H., *In Praise of Aldus Manutius.* New York: Morgan Library, 1995.
12. Charney, Noah, *The Art of Forgery: The Minds, Motives and Methods of Master Forgers.* New York: Phaedon Press, 2015.
13. Farquhar, Peter H. "Managing Brand Equity," *Marketing Research,* September 1989, 24–33.

14. Artois, Stella, https://www.stellaartois.com/en_gb/heritage.html (Accessed February 20, 2022).

15. Hudson's Bay Company, http://www.hbcheritage.ca/history/company-stories/a-brief-history-of-hbc (Accessed February 20, 2022).

16. Caswell-Murphy, https://www.caswellmassey.com/pages/our-story (Accessed February 20, 2022).

17. Ries, Al and Jack Trout, *Positioning: The Battle for Your Mind*. New York: McGraw-Hill, 1981.

18. Aaker, David A., *Managing Brand Equity*. New York: Free Press, 1991.

19. Rosenbaum-Elliott, Richard, Larry Percy, and Simon Pervan, *Strategic Brand Management*, 4th ed. Oxford: Oxford University Press, 2018.

20. John, Deborah R. and Carlos J. Torelli, *Strategic Brand Management*. Oxford: Oxford University Press, 2018.

21. Kapferrer, Jean-Noel, *Strategic Brand Management*, 2nd ed. London: Kogan-Page, 1998.

22. Keller, Kevin L. and Vanitha Swaminathan, *Strategic Brand Management*. London: Pearson, 2020, p. 29.

23. For example, see Kotler, Philip and Kevin L. Keller, *Marketing Management*. London: Pearson, 2016.

24. Weber, Joel, "Mars Inc. CEO Grant Reid is Thinking a Hundred Years Ahead," *Business Week*, January 28, 2019. https://www.bloomberg.com/news/features/2019-01-23/mars-inc-ceo-grant-reid-is-thinking-a-hundred-years-ahead.

Chapter 2

Technology Myopia*

In 1960, Ted Levitt published a classic article in the *Harvard Business Review* titled "Marketing Myopia."[1] In the article, he criticized executives for being shortsighted in how they viewed their business. More specifically, he chastised them for defining their business by the industry they were in, not by the customers they should be serving. In a similar spirit, many firms have become shortsighted in how they manage the rapid changes in the core technologies that impact their products and services in meeting customer needs. This, coupled with the consequences of fast-moving digital technologies on the entire business, can quickly make a firm vulnerable to the risk of *technology myopia*.[2]

Technology is most often viewed as the application of knowledge to make something, usually for practical use. Once a brand has achieved some status and a favorable positioning in a target market segment, it is important to maintain, if not strengthen, the brand's positioning, especially with the technology that shapes the existing product and services being offered and how consumers experience them. The challenge for managers of successful brands is the sheer *uncertainty* around new and incoming technologies and the impact on their brand and customers. Some technologies will be evolutionary and others disruptive, such as blockchain, artificial intelligence, cloud computing, or 3D printing. It is this uncertainty that leads to the need for a signpost to help reveal the possibility of technology myopia.

---

*With contributions from Chen Chen.

At least three key factors help define the signpost for myopia with regard to technology: its *velocity, visibility,* and *variety.* Difficulty in anticipating and coping with any one or combination of these driving factors can put a brand at risk.

- The *velocity* of technology can generate myopia that cripples a brand. As studied by economists, the rates at which an invention is put into practice have become shorter. This is especially the case for firms and brands that include or depend upon digital technologies, such as mobile phones, tablets, personal computers, and software, many of which have been driven by Moore's law. Basically, this law or rule of thumb is based on the observation that processing speeds in digital systems double about every two years. Although the law will reach its limits at some point, it dramatizes the influence and importance of recognizing the velocity of technology. The pervasive impact of digital technology is not only on the brand's technologies but also on the firm's business and systems processes — from development to production and operations to customer delivery.
- Many products often require a *variety* of technologies to function. This includes both the number and types of technologies, which can substantially increase the difficulty in identifying and managing them. Imagine the number of technology inputs required in the design and manufacture of an airplane and all its components. Electrical, mechanical, radar, software, sensors, fibers, and glass are a few of the many technology-based components of an aircraft. Everything must work together to function effectively. The same could be said for everyday consumer products, such as air conditioners, hair dryers, food mixers, or coffee machines. Technology myopia based on variety happens when a firm does not manage well the full array of potential technologies that can influence the performance of their brand; this includes not having enough of the right kind of technologies or juggling too many different and possibly competitive technologies.
- The *visibility* of technology, especially new ones, are critical to how a firm responds to it. If a new or oncoming technology is opaque or obscured for some reason, the time to plan a response once it is recognized can be nil. For example, and as will be seen later in this chapter, the ability for managers of smartphone brands to see the potential for touchscreen technologies put several at risk for survival.

Time is needed to recognize and digest the impact of the technology on existing products and customers, to learn it, assess resource needs, develop a plan of action, and ready the organization for response before a competitor does so.

Taken together or individually, these three factors help define the signpost for technology myopia: *Generally, for existing brands, the greater the velocity, the less visibility, and/or the greater the variety of new technologies to a firm's leadership and management, the greater the potential for technology myopia that puts a brand and its value to customers at risk.*

To illustrate the impact of technology myopia, consider VisiCalc, the first practical spreadsheet software tool for the Apple II computer launched in 1979.[3] The $99 VisiCalc innovative application developed by Dan Bricklin and Bob Frankston became an important and rapid success not only for its users who could simplify calculations with the spreadsheet, but it became a major reason for people to buy Apple's personal computers. Unfortunately, VisiCalc's success was short-lived.

In 1983, only four years later Mitch Kapor, who worked at VisiCalc, left the company to launch Lotus 1-2-3 with a greater variety of spreadsheet features for use with the emerging IBM PC technology and operating system that appealed to corporate users. Apparently, the technology changes that Kapor saw were not as visible to the key leaders at VisiCalc. VisiCalc sales dropped dramatically as the more capable Lotus 1-2-3 sales took off.

Then in 1987, Microsoft launched its Excel product, which led to the demise of Lotus and has remained a market leader for many years. The short four-year life of each of these two innovative brands was enabled by several technologies, including successive generations of speedier processors, improved operating systems, and numerous related technologies. The velocity and variety of these technologies reveal the risks of technology myopia, not only for the firms involved but also for customers who had to relearn new commands and procedures as they migrated to the different software brands.

Taken separately or together, the uncertainty created by technology velocity, visibility, and variety can create considerable risk for a firm to manage its brand. Conversely, minimizing the potential myopia by opening one's eyes to the uncertainties and carefully managing them can enable a firm to incorporate oncoming new technologies in a timely manner to better meet customer needs and maintain a strong brand.

While some might say technology myopia is obvious, as a practical matter, it should be clear that this is a very complex task for many firms to accomplish. In this chapter, Motorola and BlackBerry are two case studies in the world of mobile telephones that clearly demonstrate the problem of technology myopia and why it is an important signpost for challenges ahead. Each is considered to better understand tragedies that have befallen their once great mobile telephone brands.

Motorola: Technological Dignity at Risk

There was a time when Motorola was the monarch of mobility in telephonic communications. Its brand name was synonymous with wireless communication. However, despite its great tradition in technology, its once excellent brand in mobile phones became swamped in a sea of other brands. By 2022, Wikipedia identified more than 160 mobile phone brands globally.[4] The top five brands (Apple, Oppo, Samsung, Vivo, and Xiaomi) accounted for some 70% of all phones shipped.[5] Motorola, once the market leader, became an also-ran.

The ultimate demise came in 2011 when the company was split into two: Motorola Solutions and Motorola Mobility. Motorola Solutions continued with its focus on B2B commercial market systems and services. Motorola Mobility became the mobile phone division. It was eventually sold to Google in 2012, and then Google sold it to Lenovo in 2014, which has struggled to achieve a return on its investment.[6] Going back to its beginning helps better understand the fate of the Motorola mobile phone.

Innovator in wireless technology

Paul Galvin and his brother Joseph founded the Galvin Manufacturing Corporation in 1928.[7] From the beginning, Motorola pursued new products and technologies in the domain of wireless communication. One of its initial products was a car radio named Motorola. Galvin created the brand name to suggest sound in motion by linking "motor" (for motorcar) with "ola," from Victrola, a popular brand of phonograph at the time.[8] The company began selling its first Motorola branded radios in mid-1930. As the Great Depression from 1929 to 1939 receded, the market for automobiles grew, as did the need for car radios, including special radios for police communications and two-way mobile communicators.

In 1940, Motorola developed a hand-held two-way AM radio named the Handie-Talkie (or SCR536) that the United States military purchased and used during World War II. It was a portable radio transceiver used by the U.S. Signal Corps, accompanied by a backpack-mounted unit and nicknamed the "walkie-talkie" by troops (see Figure 2.1). Subsequently, by 1947, the Motorola car radio brand became so well-known that Galvin Manufacturing Corporation changed its name to Motorola, Inc.

Moving forward, Motorola used its research and development (R&D) capabilities to explore new technologies and develop new products.[9] In 1955, they developed the first solid-state high-power transistors and in 1957, they developed electronic paging systems that enabled individuals to be paged inside buildings that could replace noisy public address systems. More significantly, in 1983, Motorola developed the first commercial cellular phone. It was developed in cooperation with AT&T's cellular

Figure 2.1.   The SCR-300, Better Known as the Walkie-Talkie

Source: Raines, Rebecca Robins, *Getting the Message Through*. Washington, DC: Center Of Military History United States Army, 1996, p. 277. https://history.army.mil/books/30-17/Front.htm (Accessed February 27, 2023).

network over a 10-year period. Cellular communications involve a series of geographically placed towers, which create contiguous "cells" that enabled the continuous sending and receiving of radio signals located within the range of the cells. A person in possession of a portable phone, which is essentially a radio that can send and receive signals, can communicate with anyone else with a portable phone.

The so-called "mobile phone" or "cellphone" was the real beginning of modern point-to-point, anytime-anywhere communication among people. The basic human need for mobile connectivity to others outside a physical presence could be realized. The mobile phone met a variety of needs, including those related to security, socialization, and status. The early buyers of such phones were assumed to be professionals and B2B users in organizations, but it soon became evident that individual customers would find great value in mobile phones for personal use.

Motorola's first product using the cellular technology was its DynaTAC 8000 (see Figure 2.2). It weighed almost two pounds, had limited storage, required 10 hours for a recharge, and was priced at $3,995 — quite different from mobile phones in the 21st century! The innovative and popular MicroTAC[10] flip-phone followed in 1989

| (a) **DynaTAC 1983** **Analog Phone** | (b) **MicroTAC 1989** **Analog Phone** | (c) **iDEN i1000plus** **1998 Digital Phone** |

Figure 2.2.   Evolution of Major Motorola Mobile Phone Types

Source: Panels (a) and (c) from Motorola; Panel (b) from: (Redrum0486 at English Wikipedia) Via Wikimedia Commons.

(see Figure 2.2). Subsequently, the StarTAC[11] clam shell-styled phone was launched in 1996 and sold 60 million phones that year (the TAC acronym stood for Total Area Coverage). By 1998, 15 years after its initial launch, Motorola was able to leverage its strong position in cellphones to the point where it accounted for two-thirds of the company's gross revenue.[12]

During the mid-1980s, a Motorola engineer proposed the idea of a system of low orbiting satellites that would enable global communication. Ironically, it was a competitor to Motorola's own cellular technology. The firm committed to investing in the system in the late 1980s. In 1991, it spun off the project into a separate company called Iridium and by 1996, "…invested $537 million in the venture and had guaranteed $750 million in loan capacity on Iridium's behalf, the combined amount exceeding Motorola's entire profit for 1996."[13] Iridium was launched in 1998 but unfortunately failed to generate the targeted number of subscribers and revenue to cover its debt. It declared bankruptcy in August 1999, although it was subsequently resuscitated outside Motorola with operations on a limited basis.[14]

In 1991, Motorola pursued yet another internal research project culminating in the iDEN network: Integrated Digital Enhanced Network. In 1996, Nextel adopted the technology as the basis for their network system. By 1999, Motorola had developed and launched an innovative phone for this network called the iDEN i1000plus based on digital technology (see the third panel of Figure 2.2). This phone with its clamshell design was launched during 1999. As described by an industry observer:

> In 1999, Motorola once again was at the forefront of the industry, introducing the world's first smartphone with web browsing and email capabilities, the iDEN i1000plus. The handset was the first phone to combine a digital phone, two-way radio, alphanumeric pager, Internet browser, email, fax and two-way messaging.[15]

The i1000plus phone (and subsequent upgrades) was adopted primarily by professional users in the field, especially those in construction and the fire and police forces.[16] Its most popular feature was the push-to-talk capability (like the walkie-talkie) which gave this segment of the market great value. When Nextel was acquired by Sprint in 2004, the iDEN network was abandoned, which effectively ended the life of the Motorola series of iDEN phones.

In addition to their leadership position in hand-held cellphones, Motorola generated revenue from equipment and services provided to base station offices and towers that enabled cellular communication. The firm was developing and offering a large variety of technologies in their phones and networks, some of which were overlapping. Nevertheless, by 1998–1999, few would disagree that Motorola was the brand leader in the world of mobile communication.

How technology myopia put Motorola at risk

Some brand tragedies can happen without warning. Others have numerous indicators or flaws that are either missed or dismissed and represent serious missteps in maintaining the brand's strength. In the case of Motorola, the *variety* and *velocity* of technologies employed may have seriously contributed to its demise in the mobile phone market. Essentially, Motorola was fielding at least four different and overlapping communication technologies: paging, cellular, iDEN, and satellite. It was competing with itself by accelerating the development of multiple technologies. The firm's desire to be at the forefront of each and all of these mobile technologies created a myopia that distracted investments to better meet customer needs in the growing cellular business.

For example, in 1998, Nokia became the first mobile telephone brand to overtake Motorola in market share as the number one mobile phone. This should have been sufficient indication that Motorola needed to rethink its approach to the mobile communication market. Nokia's success was based on its digital technology and design. Benefits of digital included lower power requirements and more efficient storage of any data translated, including human voice which can be used to save and reproduce voice messages. Ironically, Motorola possessed such digital technology in its i1000plus phone, but it was offered through Nextel to a smaller market segment than the overall mobile phone market. They did not manage to change to digital until competitors gained a strong advantage ... too late to become competitive.

The second competitor to Motorola's cellular phone business was Research In Motion (RIM), which ultimately became BlackBerry (to be covered subsequently in this chapter). During the period of 1996–1999, RIM focused on sending and receiving messages primarily through paging technology. Motorola, which developed the first electronic pagers, saw them strictly as a specific application of that technology rather than the need it met for users. Nevertheless, the myopia in not carefully monitoring Nokia's digital technology and RIM's evolution from an email pager to a full-fledged phone with a keyboard for sending and receiving messages put Motorola in a vulnerable market position. Seeing and acting more aggressively on these early RIM technology trends may have better prepared them for the ultimate success of the BlackBerry 5810 series, which launched in 2002. These missteps by Motorola were seen as a weakness in anticipating and responding to technology trends:

> Moreover, the company had experienced several previous business mishaps, including a failure to anticipate the cellular industry's switch to digital cell phones, which played a major role in Motorola's more than 50% share price decline in 1998.[17]

The consequence of focusing primarily on a variety of new technologies and not carefully understanding their relative value to customers put Motorola's brand at risk. Customers looked to other brands to better meet their needs, such as Nokia and BlackBerry in the late 1990s and early 2000s. Ultimately, the Motorola brand of mobile phones was sold to and marketed by Lenovo as a less expensive phone, yet with good features. Going into the 2020s, its global market share was relatively low (about 3%), which was minimal compared to its glory days. The monarch of mobility surrendered its throne to others.

BlackBerry: Getting into a Technology Jam

Going into the year 2000, Motorola was the dominant competitor in the overall mobile communications market. Nokia with its digital technology held a slight market share lead over Motorola in the cellphone market, but Motorola was stronger across a variety of devices, including electronic pagers. Mike Lazaridis and Jim Balsillie, co-CEOs of RIM, focused their early development efforts on the pager market, which ultimately evolved into the BlackBerry phone that became the most popular device on the market for the majority of the first 10 years of the 21st century.

The brand name was chosen due to the similarities between the keyboard's buttons and the characteristics of the blackberry fruit. The phone was so popular that users appeared addicted to them, some even calling it the "CrackBerry." Its rise to success was spectacular in many ways. Unfortunately, the brand began to unravel with its customers after a major BlackBerry operating system crash during October 2011. From Monday morning October 10, 2011 until Thursday morning October 13, 2011, BlackBerry suffered a rolling global outage of its operating system.[18] No one who owned a BlackBerry could use it. Its technology failed. It was the beginning of a series of challenges for the BlackBerry brand and its relationship with customers.

This outage was not the only rough spot in the brand's performance; there were previous email and other outages from 2007 to 2010. However, the breakdown in 2011 resulted in numerous customers leaving BlackBerry for rising competitors and placing it in a critical financial position. By the end of 2011, BlackBerry was losing market share and its stock price was $15, down from $58 at the end of 2010 — a 75% decline. The board of directors of the firm wanted a change in management. In January 2012, the co-CEOs Mike Lazaridis and Jim Balsillie stepped down from their positions relinquishing control to a new CEO.[19]

The birth and growth of BlackBerry

Mike Lazaridis and Doug Fregin founded RIM in Waterloo, Ontario, in 1984. After a series of developing various kinds of electronic product offerings, they became enchanted with a new product from Ericsson in Sweden called Mobitex. It was essentially a wireless network that moved data across radio waves, an idea that would drive Lazaridis to consider a product that could be developed to meet user needs. For example, he believed it would be of great value for business firms to connect with their out-of-office employees, such as drivers, salespeople, and managers during working hours.

Jim Balsillie was hired in 1992 as co-CEO with Lazaridis. Lazaridis was more the technology driver and Balsillie the business driver. As noted in the book *Losing the Signal*,[20] it was clear that each had quite different personalities resulting in both positive and negative consequences for the relationship. Nevertheless, the two worked together to create a series of breakthrough products during the 1990s and beyond.

Their first four products were pagers that enabled two-way communication via text messages. One of these, the model 850 launched in January 1999, was the first to enable interactive emails and carry the

(a) **RIM Pager**	(b) **BlackBerry Phone**	(c) **BlackBerry-Bold Phone**
Model 950-1998*	Model 8700-2004**	Model 9650-2010***

Figure 2.3.   Evolution of Selected BlackBerry Mobile Phones

Source: (a) Wikimedia Commons, by Ruben de Rijcke — Own work, CC BY-SA 4.0, https://
commons.wikimedia.org/w/index.php?curid=77870601. (b) By Robert J. Thomas — Own work of
own phone. (c) Wikimedia Commons, by Evan-Amos — Own work, Public Domain, https://
commons.wikimedia.org/w/index.php?curid=16116551.

BlackBerry name. The first true BlackBerry "smart" phone, the 5810, arrived in the United States on March 4, 2002.[21] Successive new models arrived after the 5810 with improved features — the 6230 (also the Quark) was very popular among corporate users and in 2006, the Pearl became very popular among customers with its camera and media player (see Figure 2.3 for an evolutionary illustration of selected models).[22] By 2007, BlackBerry had become a well-established brand among corporate users and customers. BlackBerry's advantage over the dominant Motorola cellphone was that it provided users with tremendous mobile productivity via email communications with its full keyboard, a cellular phone, a basic set of applications, and importantly, system security.

The maturation and decline of BlackBerry

The launch of the Apple iPhone in 2007 sent shock waves throughout the industry. Steve Jobs made it very clear that BlackBerry was a major target.

Apple's iPhone, he promised, wouldn't come with the frustrating "fixed" or "plastic" keyboards that made Internet navigation so cumbersome. "We are going to … get rid of all these buttons and use this giant screen," he said waving an iPhone at his audience.[23]

Both Lazaridis and Balsillie were surprised by the announcement. Unfortunately, it was reported the co-CEOs did not initially see the threat as a serious one:

RIM's chiefs didn't give much additional thought to Apple for months. 'It wasn't a threat to RIM's core business,' says Lazaridis's top lieutenant, Larry Conlee. 'It wasn't secure. It had rapid battery drain and a lousy [digital] keyboard.' If the iPhone gained traction, RIM's senior executives believed, it would be with customers who cared more about YouTube and other Internet escapes than efficiency and security.[24]

In hindsight, Steve Jobs and Apple's special style of marketing communication with customers effectively took a sledgehammer to the wall of BlackBerry's successful brand.

With the launch of the iPhone, BlackBerry began to lose market share. The first and second quarter financials of 2008 revealed this weakness and by October 2008, it was widely reported that iPhone surpassed BlackBerry in sales.[25] The stock price at the end of 2007 was $113, and by the end of 2008, it was $41. While this could be partly attributed to an oncoming recession at the end of 2008, the impact of Apple and its new technologies were substantial. From 2008 until 2011, BlackBerry struggled to regain sales and market share, but the network system outage in October 2011 seriously damaged the credibility of the BlackBerry brand and its relationship with customers leading to further declines (see the highlighted vertical ovals in the top part of Figure 2.4).

Mike Lazaridis was always proud of RIM's ability to respond to changes in technology that kept it one step ahead of competition. But this ability unraveled in response to Apple's iPhone. Several months after the iPhone launch, RIM finally realized that Apple was a very serious threat to all parts of its business. Lazaridis and the BlackBerry R&D team went to work on the next BlackBerry called Storm to meet the iPhone's ascent.

Lazaridis and Balsillie were committed to their innovative physical action thumb keyboards. It was undoubtedly a major contributor to its initial successes and hard to let go, not only by users but also by the

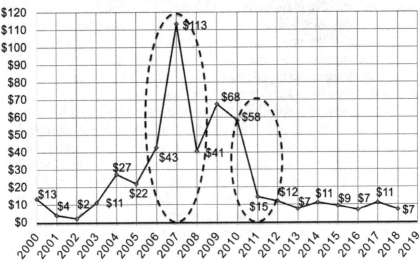

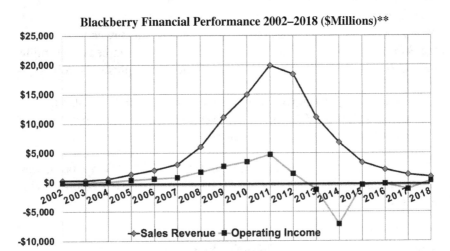

Figure 2.4.   BlackBerry Stock Price and Financials

Source: *Data adjusted for splits, obtained from: https://www.macrotrends.net/stocks/charts/BB/blackberry/stock-price-history.

**Wikipedia contributors, "BlackBerry Limited," *Wikipedia, The Free Encyclopedia*. https://en.wikipedia.org/w/index.php?title=BlackBerry_Limited&oldid=906421559 (Accessed July 28, 2019).

BlackBerry team. The Apple iPhone had no such tactile keyboard; it relied on a touch-sensitive glass keyboard that at first was problematic for users but rapidly improved with subsequent generations of its phone. The intent of the design of the new BlackBerry Storm was also to use a total glass surface for the phone but maintain its traditional tactile keyboard. The technology designed to do this was a glass surface that could emulate the click and feel of BlackBerry's traditional keyboard.

Working to meet a deadline for a large phone contract with Verizon, its main carrier, Lazaridis pushed his research and development team hard to meet an end-of-the-year 2008 deadline to launch Storm. However, during development, the Storm experienced numerous technical issues, including the glass-sensitive touchscreen keyboard that did not work consistently. Despite concerns among BlackBerry's own R&D team and early negative reviews of the Storm by external tech reviewers, the launch proceeded in November 2008 to meet the requirements of its network provider, Verizon.

With heavy marketing by BlackBerry and Verizon, customers bought the Storm in large numbers through the Verizon network. The BlackBerry name carried a strong measure of trust among its users and potential users, which supported the sales response. Unfortunately, the dire concerns about the Storm's technical performance were true. Customers began returning their phones to Verizon stores asking for replacement phones or refunds:

> Virtually, every one of the first batch of about 1 million Storms shipped needed replacing. Many of the replacements were being returned as well. The Storm was a complete failure. …[26]

This technological failure alone did not doom BlackBerry, but it was yet another serious setback that was clearly problematic for the brand with its customers.

The BlackBerry brand: Living in the shadows

Similar to the stock price chart, the lower part of Figure 2.4 shows the dramatic rise and fall in BlackBerry sales revenue and net operating income (EBIT) from 2002 to 2018, with the values peaking in 2011. The global active user base peaked at 80 million users in 2012, declining to 56 million in 2014, and to 16 million users by 2016.[27] In 2011, RIM employed some 19,000 people; by 2017, only 4,044 people were employed. After the two co-CEO's resigned at the end of 2011, Thorsten

Heins replaced them. Heins focused on the January 2013 launch of the BlackBerry 10 operating system. Despite a favorable reception of the new operating system, the BlackBerry mobile phone was further challenged by the increasingly competitive market, including iPhone, and the rise of Google's Android-based operating system phones.

In November 2014, Heins was replaced by John Chen as CEO. Under Chen's leadership, BlackBerry shifted its focus primarily to enterprise services that provided secure data and communication to users. In 2016, BlackBerry discontinued manufacturing its phones, however it licensed the brand and technology to TCL Communication in 2017, although this relationship ended in 2020. Then, on January 4, 2022, the company announced that it "decommissioned the infrastructure and services used by our legacy software and phone operating systems which are over 20 years old now."[28] Blackberry phones using the Android operating system should still work and rumors abound for a 5G version of the BlackBerry to emerge in the 2020s. That the BlackBerry brand is not dead and lives on is a testament to its strength among a segment of customers. However, its powerful brand recognition with a larger end user customer base was badly damaged, possibly beyond repair. As noted by one industry observer back in 2011:

> It should be evident by now that a corporate tragedy is under way at the proud Canadian firm Research In Motion.... The manner in which the firm has now squandered the early technological lead and brand recognition it had in BlackBerry mobile-email devices is astonishing.[29]

Coping With Technology Myopia

Motorola and BlackBerry in the mobile telephone market provide valuable case studies in better understanding how technology myopia can result in brand tragedies. Could Motorola managers have seen BlackBerry's superior email messaging technology coming and responded in anticipation of it with their own new product? Could BlackBerry have foreseen the launch of Apple's iPhone with its new touchscreen technology? While definitive answers are not possible, the three technology myopia factors of velocity, visibility, and variety help explain these unfortunate brand tragedies.

In the case of Motorola, it is evident that by 1998 they possessed the technology to see the potential threat of a BlackBerry on the horizon, but if they did, they took little or no action. Motorola was the technology leader in mobile communication on several platforms. In addition to its game-changing cellular system, it had its paging technology, its iDEN network with the innovative i1000plus digital phone, and its satellite-based Iridium system. All their technologies were at the core of mobile communication. But when you are distracted by a large *variety* of high *velocity* technologies, whether your own or from others, you plant the seeds of myopia and run the risk of losing sight of the technologies that are driving market needs — in this case, BlackBerry's network.

BlackBerry's success with early corporate customers grew because of the need it met with the superior security technology provided by its operating system. The BlackBerry OS and the BlackBerry Enterprise Server (BES) with regular upgrades continued from its launch in January 1999 to January 2013.[30] Its earliest versions were very basic, relying on the Java programming language and computing platform and its own encrypted security capabilities. This effectively supported corporations and governments that wanted secure communication capabilities. Though limited in its overall capacity, RIM was strongly committed to its existing network and network strategy. Ironically, this strength over Motorola may have eventually made the firm's leaders oblivious to other network technologies.

From its beginning, BlackBerry's technology strategy thrived on conserving network capacity to deliver messages and other capabilities securely through its devices. Alternatively, Apple and eventually Google viewed the network as a much more dynamic and an ever-expanding capability to support the growing number of users and their needs. They viewed the mobile phone as an extension of the personal computer that could do almost anything online. BlackBerry viewed the mobile phone as a secure email messaging device but eventually had to change this view as market needs shifted. BlackBerry's myopic commitment to one form of network technology distracted their *visibility* of the dramatically changing network technology situation among users in their customer base.

Another available technology that was apparently not *visible* to Blackberry, Motorola, and other emerging competitors was the mobile phone touchscreen. Everyone seemed to have been taken by surprise with Apple's announcement of the iPhone and its touchscreen surface that gave buyers fingertip accessibility to a variety of applications, but it should not have been a surprise! Among the first touchscreen devices was the

Elograph, developed by Samuel Hurst in 1971.[31] By 1977, working with Siemens, Hurst created what is considered the first true touchscreen device called the Accutouch. Later, in 1982, at the University of Toronto in Canada (ironically, one-and-a-half hours by car east of Waterloo, Ontario, the home of BlackBerry), multi-touchscreen technology was developed by Nimish Mehta. Furthermore, as noted by Saffer:

> More than a decade before Apple released the iPhone.... IBM and Bell South launched Simon, a touchscreen mobile phone. It was ahead of its time and never caught on, but it demonstrated that a mobile touchscreen could be manufactured and sold.[32]

Although the Simon, launched in 1994, had touchscreen capabilities, some features of the screen design made it difficult to use. It is also worth noting that Apple used touchscreen technology on its failed Newton personal digital assistant, launched in 1993 and terminated in 1998. The touchscreen technology signpost for BlackBerry and others was ahead but missed or dismissed: a clear case of technology myopia based on the *visibility* factor. BlackBerry belatedly responded with the Storm, but it failed because its design could not retain the true feel of a mechanical keyboard. BlackBerry could not easily abandon what made them so successful in the first place: its QWERTY keyboard. Finally, Motorola and Blackberry's technology myopia leading to their tragedies may have also been linked to a strong belief in their own successes and often the hubris that accompanies it, to be addressed further in Chapters 6 and 7.

Another troubling miss for BlackBerry may have been the overlooked value for users Apple brought with its *variety* of downloadable software applications (Apps). In July 2008, Apple launched its App Store, which enabled customers to download productivity software, games, and other kinds of applications to meet their individual needs. In the first month of its existence, some 60 million apps were downloaded by iPhone customers.[33] While this stressed network capabilities, the AT&T's and Verizon's of the world began expanding their capacity to meet and capitalize on those needs. This increased the urgency for BlackBerry to improve its phone Internet browser capabilities and develop a wide variety of apps. Unfortunately, RIM's myopia with regard to app variety to meet customer's needs set the stage for additional problems:

> Meanwhile, the rush to sell consumer apps exposed one of RIM's glaring shortcomings: it had never adequately invested in software tools or

offered much support to outside developers, which frustrated many who tried to write programs for BlackBerry.[34]

Propositions to Consider in Developing a Signpost for Technology Myopia

In retrospect, the signposts for tragedies at firms such as Motorola, BlackBerry, and others may be apparent. However, detecting them is not always easy. To help other brand providers develop signposts, throughout the remaining chapters in this book, several sets of propositions are presented to stimulate their consideration and development. The immediate purpose of these propositions is not to uncover and explain all these complexities but to build awareness and commitment among brand leaders and managers to continuously explore their implicit and explicit vulnerabilities to a brand tragedy that can harm brand equity.

Based on the case studies presented in this chapter, three summary propositions for the signpost of technology myopia are proposed on three key factors: velocity, variety, and visibility. Behind each of these propositions and their interactions are numerous complexities about the technologies that can influence an organization and its customers in a market. The propositions are merely summary statements of these complexities.

- **Velocity:** The greater the *velocity* of technology change in a market, the greater the vulnerability to a brand tragedy.
- **Variety:** The greater the *variety* of new technologies that influence a market, the greater the vulnerability to a brand tragedy.
- **Visibility:** The less *visibility* of new and relevant technologies in a market, the greater the vulnerability to a brand tragedy.

When technology myopia — whether too much, too fast, or not apparent — gives a competitor a clear advantage that provides real customer value, it is very difficult to win back lost customers. Brand loyalty developed with customers can be shattered. It's possible that some segments of customers will retain loyalty (Motorola and BlackBerry eventually sold their mobile brands to others), but technology myopia made its original value very difficult to restore. The importance of customer loyalty and how to manage it once it has been damaged will be considered further in Chapter 3.

Endnotes

1. Levitt, Theodore, "Marketing Myopia," *Harvard Business Review*, 38(4), July–August 1960, 45–56.
2. Wyman, John, "SMR Forum: Technology Myopia-The Need to Think Strategically About Technology," *Sloan Management Review*, 26(4), Summer 1985, 59–64.
3. For additional detail see: Burton, Grad, "The Creation and the Demise of VisiCalc," *IEEE Annals of the History of Computing*, 29:3, July–September 2007, 20–31.
4. Wikipedia contributors, "List of Mobile Phone Brands by Country," *Wikipedia, The Free Encyclopedia.* https://en.wikipedia.org/w/index.php?title=List_of_mobile_phone_brands_by_country&direction=next&oldid=958105596#Active_list (Accessed May 4, 2022).
5. IDC Quarterly Mobile Phone Tracker, Q4 2021, January 27, 2022, https://www.idc.com/getdoc.jsp?containerId=prUS48830822 (Accessed May 4, 2022).
6. Jennings, Ralph, "How China's Tech Giant Lenovo is Losing its Grip on Smartphones," *Forbes*, April 3, 2018, https://www.forbes.com/sites/ralphjennings/2018/04/03/how-chinas-tech-giant-lenovo-is-losing-its-grip-on-smartphones/#1b6259fe128e.
7. For background on Paul Galvin see Petrakis, Harry M., *The Founder's Touch*. New York: McGraw-Hill, 1965.
8. "Sound in Motion," https://www.motorolasolutions.com/en_us/about/company-overview/history/explore-motorola-heritage/sound-motion.html (Accessed May 4, 2022).
9. Motorola Solutions History, https://www.motorolasolutions.com/en_xu/about/company-overview/history.html (Accessed May 4, 2022).
10. Wikipedia contributors, "Motorola MicroTAC," *Wikipedia, The Free Encyclopedia.* https://en.wikipedia.org/w/index.php?title=Motorola_MicroTAC&oldid=1058650133 (Accessed May 4, 2022).
11. Wikipedia contributors, "Motorola StarTAC," *Wikipedia, The Free Encyclopedia.* https://en.wikipedia.org/w/index.php?title=Motorola_StarTAC&oldid=906372505 (Accessed May 4, 2022).
12. Mitchell, John F., "Time Magazine Milestones section," *Time Magazine*, July 6, 2009, p. 17.
13. Collins, James C., *How The Mighty Fall: And Why Some Companies Never Give In*. New York, NY: HarperCollins Publishers, 2009.

14. Mellow, Craig, "The Rise and Fall and Rise of Iridium," *Air & Space Magazine*, September 2004, https://www.smithsonianmag.com/air-space-magazine/the-rise-and-fall-and-rise-of-iridium-5615034/ (Accessed May 4, 2022).

15. Messieh, Nancy, "15 Facts You May Not Know About Motorola," *thenextweb.com*, August 15, 2011, https://thenextweb.com/mobile/2011/08/15/15-facts-you-may-not-know-about-motorola/ (Accessed May 4, 2022).

16. Lawson, Stephen, "Sprint's iDEN Finally Headed for Sign-Off," *Computerworld*, December 7, 2010, https://www.computerworld.com/article/2514783/sprint-s-iden-finally-headed-for-sign-off.html (Accessed May 4, 2022).

17. Finkelstein, Sydney and Shade H. Sanford, "Learning from Corporate Mistakes: The Rise and Fall of Iridium," *Organizational Dynamics*, 29(2), 138–148.

18. Pepitone, Julianne, "BlackBerry Service Restored After Worst Outage Ever," *CNN Money*, October 13, 2011, https://money.cnn.com/2011/10/13/technology/blackberry_outage/index.htm (Accessed May 4, 2022).

19. For a comprehensive and detailed description of the BlackBerry story see: McNish, Jacquie and Sean Silcoff, *Losing the Signal: The Untold Story Behind the Extraordinary Rise and Spectacular Fall of BlackBerry*. New York, NY: Flatiron Books, 2018.

20. *Ibid.*

21. It's a Phone! It's a Pager! It's a BlackBerry! *ExtremeTech.com*, March 4, 2002. https://www.extremetech.com/extreme/73146-its-a-phone-its-a-pager-its-a-BlackBerry (Accessed July 25, 2019).

22. For additional models of Black-Berrymobile phones see https://www.zdnet.com/pictures/photos-blackberrys-through-the-ages/2/.

23. McNish and Silcoff, *Op. cit.*, p. 130.

24. *Ibid.*, p. 133.

25. "iPhone Passes BlackBerry in 3Q Sales," *UPI*, November 8, 2008, https://www.upi.com/Business_News/2008/11/08/iPhone-passes-Blackberry-in-3Q-sales/93651226174741/ (Accessed May 4, 2022).

26. *Ibid.*, p. 166.

27. Wikipedia contributors, "BlackBerry," *Wikipedia, The Free Encyclopedia*. https://en.wikipedia.org/w/index.php?title=BlackBerry&oldid=1084318834 (Accessed May 4, 2022).

28. Chen, John, "BlackBerry's Transformation Journey and Our Smartphone Heritage," Janurary 4, 2022, https://blogs.blackberry.com/en/2022/01/blackberrys-transformation-journey-and-our-smartphone-heritage (Accessed May 4, 2022).

29. Peers, Martin, "BlackBerry Maker's Slow-Motion Decline," *Wall Street Journal*, March 25, 2011.

30. Woods, Ben, "The Road to BlackBerry 10: The Evolution of RIM's OS and BES," ZDNet.com, January 24, 2013, https://www.zdnet.com/article/the-road-to-blackberry-10-the-evolution-of-rims-os-and-bes/ (Accessed May 4, 2022).

31. For a history and explanation of touchscreens, see: Saffer, Dan, *Designing Gestural Interfaces: Touchscreens and Interactive Devices.* Sebastopol, CA: O'Reilly Media, Inc., 2009.

32. Saffer, *Op. cit.*, p. 10.

33. Wingfield, Nick, "iPhone Software Sales Take Off: Apple's Jobs," *Wall Street Journal*, August 11, 2008, https://www.wsj.com/articles/SB121842341491928977.

34. McNish and Silcoff, *Op. cit.*, p. 171.

Chapter 3

Ruptured Loyalties*

Loyalty is a powerful concept. Being loyal is an act of giving. "Loyal" is defined as "giving or showing firm and constant support or allegiance to a person or institution.[1]" When business and marketing people talk about "brand" loyalty, they are typically talking about a customer's loyalty to their brand. Unfortunately, when talking about brand loyalty, very few business and marketing people talk about their loyalty to the customer. What does an organization give in the way of support and allegiance to show it too is loyal to its customers? Do so-called "loyalty programs" meet the test of showing firm and constant support to customers? Loyalty exists within the customer and within the brand provider. How they define their mutual relationships with each other can make or break a brand.

Sadly, this is not the traditional view of loyalty in most business and marketing contexts. The American Marketing Association defines brand loyalty as repeat purchasing[2]:

> Brand loyalty is a situation in which a consumer generally buys the same manufacturer-originated product or service repeatedly over time rather than buying from multiple suppliers within the category. It is the degree to which a consumer consistently purchases the same brand within a product class.

While repeat purchasing is an important indicator of customer loyalty to a brand, it only represents one dimension of it: purchasing behavior. It

---

*With Contributions from Morgan Swedberg Seymour.

ignores the drivers of that behavior and its consequences. Loyalty is more complex than simply viewing it as a person's series of transactions. This complexity, and how well it is understood, can have important implications for brands and therefore becomes a critical signpost for a brand's strength and vulnerability to a tragedy.

Consider the case of customers who attain a certain desirable status as frequent flyers in an airline's frequent flyer program. However, they soon realize that when they don't fly as often or reach a certain dollar amount of spending, they lose that status. The loss of a certain desired status in a loyalty program reveals to customers that it is loyalty based solely on transactions, not that the company is loyal or cares about them in a non-financial way. This can put a customer's brand relationship at risk.

The key learning point of this chapter is that loyalty in a business or any other context is a two-way street. It is proposed that a customer's loyalty to a brand is more about a brand provider's demonstrated loyalty to a customer than just a purchase. It represents a signpost that can lead to a long-term favorable relationship or a tragic outcome.

Deeper Insights Into Loyalty

Loyalty is the outcome of a relationship between and among parties who evidence consistent support and allegiance to each other. The relationship involves interactions of a person's **cognitive**, **affective**, and **behavioral** domains, as shown in the three Borromean circles in Figure 3.1. It is about what people *think*, *feel*, and *do* with regard to a brand. While the Borromean circle is a mathematical concept in topology, it has been used to show the interdependency of trinities in religion, coats of arms, and even brand logos.

The representation of the *cognitive* (think), *affective* (feel), and *behavioral* (do) domains is widely accepted and studied in psychology,[3] as well as in marketing and consumer behavior to better understand attitudes.[4] It is applied here to better grasp the meaning of loyalty. The underlying proposition of the three domains represented as Borromean circles is that all must be present in an ongoing relationship to experience loyalty; removing any one domain puts loyalty at risk. Furthermore, even though brand loyalty is typically associated with customer behavior, in this chapter, serious consideration is given to the importance of ways that a brand provider can demonstrate their loyalty to customers.

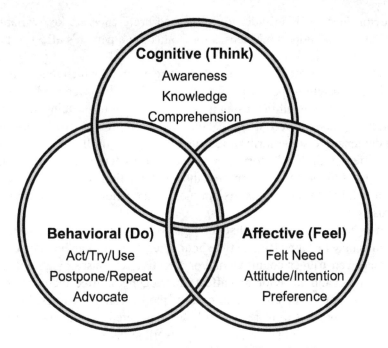

Figure 3.1.   Three Domains of Loyalty and Illustrative Measures

The **cognitive** domain involves the "mental action or process of acquiring knowledge and understanding through thought, experience, and the senses."[5] This includes how a person becomes aware of something, such as a brand, how they acquire knowledge about it, and the extent to which they comprehend its meaning and form beliefs about it. Awareness, knowledge, and comprehension become important variables that help define key metrics for assessing the cognitive domain for a brand. Practically, a brand cannot begin to exist in a person, or people in a brand provider's organization, without at least awareness.

The **affective** domain relates to "moods, feelings, and attitudes."[6] This is an important function as it involves predispositions to behave. It can be seen as the connection between the cognitive and behavioral domains. For example, awareness and comprehension of information via the cognitive domain may activate a felt need, which in turn may lead to behavior. Alternatively, the information gathered that triggers a felt need may be inadequate and require additional information search until an attitude is formed and a preference is established possibly leading to a certain behavior. Felt need, attitude, intention, and preference are key variables that help define important metrics for evaluating a person's affect or pre-disposition to act.

The **behavioral** domain involves "the way in which one acts or conducts oneself, especially toward others."[7] Actions can take many forms — trying something, using it, postponing action, speaking to others, or in many cases, doing nothing. Actions also represent overt behaviors that demonstrate some form of resource allocation. In the context of loy-alty, different kinds of efforts can be extended to demonstrate strong and consistent support for one or more others in a relationship: the true mean-ing of loyalty. As the popular axiom indicates, "actions speak louder than words."

It is important to note that for loyalty to exist, each of these three domains may be tapped at one time or another, and they can be interactive. Behavior can trigger cognitive and/or affective responses, cognition can trigger affect and behavior, and affect can trigger cognitive and behavioral responses. This is the conceptual basis of the Borromean circles. In addi-tion, for the process to work, it should be considered from the perspective of a customer as well as for people who work at brand providers.

Customers who are loyal to a brand may show it in many ways. They may be open to information about the brand from many sources, their feelings toward the brand may intensify or diminish, their purchasing may increase or decrease, and their communication with others may change based on their experiences with the brand. Typically, customers will also respond favorably to loyalty programs that meet their needs. Such pro-grams are one way a firm can communicate its loyalty. The use of various customer satisfaction measures in surveys, such as the Net Promoter Score,[8] is often to provide a reading on this key topic.

Brand providers who want to show customers their loyalty through their brand can do it in many ways. A firm has one or more managers and employees with cognitive, affective, and behavioral domains that can be focused on customers. These managerial decision domains are often rep-resented in terms of market research and related methods to better under-stand customers and their needs (cognitive domain), selecting a preferred segment of customers on which to focus to meet their needs better than competitors (affective domain), and applying resources to implement marketing communications and loyalty programs to gain purchase and advocacy for their brand (behavioral domain).

For brand providers this often means increased support for people in customer service, technical support, and the sales force who directly inter-act with customers. It is sometimes incredible that brand providers, espe-cially business firms, don't grasp the entire scope and value of the dynamics of reciprocal customer loyalty as a signpost that can signal a threat to their brands, as the following case studies demonstrate.

Tropicana Puts the Squeeze on Customer Loyalty

It is reported that oranges arrived in America around 1560 when explorers from Spain landed in Florida and brought orange trees to be planted and grown.[9] It is also reported that Spanish missionaries brought a different orange variety to California in the 1700s.[10] The popular California "navel" oranges were typically peeled and eaten fresh. However, in the early 1900s, abundant crops often provided an excess supply of oranges that motivated a desire among growers to sell more to customers. In 1905, the growers formed the California Orange Growers Exchange (subsequently renamed to Sunkist Growers, Inc.) and sought to increase demand for their oranges by recruiting ad agencies to propose marketing programs.

In 1916, the Exchange awarded Albert Lasker and his ad agency the opportunity to launch a marketing communications campaign for custom-ers. The chosen creative approach was to encourage customers to squeeze oranges at home and enjoy fresh orange juice. An example of one such ad was "Drink an Orange," which was placed on the last page of the then popular *Saturday Evening Post* (see Figure 3.2).[11] The ad also informed customers they could purchase a newly developed orange juice extractor for only 10 cents to squeeze fresh juice. In effect, the campaign not only sold oranges but also stimulated the emergence of a relatively new cate-gory: fresh orange juice. As a result, substantially, more oranges were consumed because it took two to three oranges to make a glass of juice. The campaign also promoted health themes as reasons why it was impor-tant to consume oranges and orange juice.

Seeing the California success, orange growers in Florida took up the process of making juice from their oranges, which were difficult to peel, but sweeter and juicier — perfect for orange juice. While squeezing fresh oranges was compelling, it was not as convenient as the emergence of

Figure 3.2.   "Drink an Orange" Ad

Source: *Saturday Evening Post*, February 19, 1916, p. 76.

canned orange juice, which despite its poorer taste could be distributed and sold in grocery stores. However, the breakthrough in orange juice sales began in 1946 with the introduction of the Minute Maid brand of frozen concentrate from Florida oranges, made by a Florida firm called Vacuum Foods. It resulted from a research program begun during World War II to provide better tasting and accessible vitamin C for the military. Orange juice was made by opening the package of frozen contents and stirring it into a pitcher of water. The challenge was how to communicate this consumption experience to American customers.

The eventual success of orange juice from frozen concentrate has been attributed to a communication campaign featuring Bing Crosby, a top box office American actor and crooner. Crosby promoted the benefits of the new Minute Maid brand of frozen concentrate on a weekly radio program called *This is Bing Crosby*.[12] At the time, crooning was a very popular form of singing that could be interpreted as somewhat soothing for Americans after years of war in the early 1940s and the uncertainty about the future it brought.

The radio program involved 15 minutes of recorded songs and conversation between Bing Crosby and a host about the new product. This occurred five days a week. During the program, Crosby discussed the benefits of orange juice along with the ease of preparation from the frozen concentrate. Crosby was the trusted voice of the brand that spoke to consumers. Sales of Minute Maid accelerated through the 1950s! In 1960, the Coca-Cola company purchased Minute Maid and used its marketing prowess to further stimulate sales of the frozen concentrate.

In another part of Florida, Tropicana Products, Inc. was founded in 1947 by Anthony Rossi.[13] Convinced that ready-to-consume fresh orange juice tasted better and was more convenient, he set out to develop such a product. In 1954, using the process of flash pasteurization, Rossi was able to develop a not-from-concentrate product that could be made available to customers by truck and train in a chilled ready-to-serve package. Branded as Tropicana Pure Premium, the product was well received by customers. Sales grew rapidly and overtook Coca-Cola's Minute Maid frozen from concentrate brand. Seagram acquired Tropicana in 1988 and eventually sold it to PepsiCo in 1998. The Tropicana brand became almost synonymous with fresh Florida orange juice.

Customers valued and trusted the Tropicana brand for its wide avail-ability, product consistency, and package visibility, which gave it a strong market share against major competitors. A reporter from the *Orlando Sentinel* newspaper observed a typical supermarket shopper in Orlando who "walked up to the orange juice display, spotted the rows of Tropicana cartons, and promptly snatched one from the shelf. No hesitation. No bar-gain shopping." Upon being interviewed, the customer indicated "she would not even consider buying another brand .... I like the taste of it, I like their ads. I like the way they package it. I feel like I'm drinking some-thing natural."[14] Here is a customer demonstrating cognitive, affective, and behavioral responses that revealed relatively strong loyalty to the brand.

Going into the 1990s, the orange juice industry grew steadily, along with substantial production capacity. PepsiCo's Tropicana was the market leader followed by Coca-Cola's Minute Maid, which also introduced a fresh packaged orange juice brand in 2001 (Simply Orange) as a competi-tor. Throughout this time, a variety of regulatory interventions monitored and contested the health and quality aspects of orange juice and commu-nication about it.[15]

Beginning in the late 1990s, American customers began to become more health-conscious and concerned with sugar consumption. While orange juice contained substantial amounts of vitamin C, it also included sugar. Consequently, sales began to fall in the early 2000s (see Figure 3.3). In addition to the decline in sales, private label competitors arose putting pressure on prices and setting the stage for confrontation between the two major brands of orange juice: Tropicana and Minute Maid. It also set the stage for Tropicana to commit a marketing blunder that put their trusted brand at risk with customers.

A marketing misstep

Faced with declining sales going into 2008 and the impact of the major recession beginning December 2007 and lasting until 2009, Tropicana engaged an external agency to advise on how to improve its situation. Tropicana managers accepted the agency's recommended strategy of rebranding Tropicana with an emphasis on modernizing the look of the packaging, along with a new tagline for its advertising. The objective was to reignite customer interest in the brand. The Tropicana rebranding came in the form of an updated logo and packaging for the orange juice.

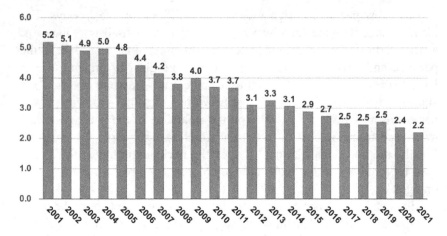

Figure 3.3.   U.S. Per Capita Consumption of Orange Juice in Gallons

Source: Based on data from Kramer, Jaclyn, Skyler Simnitt, and Catharine Weber, *Fruit and Tree Nuts Outlook: March 2022*, FTS-374, U.S. Department of Agriculture, Economic Research Service, March 30, 2022. (Data are for amounts ending in September of each growing year.)

The new campaign launched on January 9, 2009, with a cost estimated at $35 million. Customer response and sales plummeted almost immediately. By February 22, 2009, Tropicana orange juice unit sales fell by 20% with a $33 million decline in dollar sales, while sales for the entire refrigerated-orange-juice category did not change.[16] During this time, Minute Maid and other competitors experienced double-digit sales increases, largely from the defection of Tropicana customers.   What happened?

The customer's shopping experience for Tropicana changed from the familiar to the unfamiliar. The front face of the original Tropicana package included its iconic large orange with a red and white striped straw sticking out of it at a 45-degree angle. Visually the orange and the straw were inviting and appeared ready for sipping. The classic arching Tropicana logo in dark leafy green was placed just above the iconic orange with the straw. The sub-logo of "Pure Premium" appeared in much smaller print below the large Tropicana brand name. Together they were centered on the face of the package, almost covering it horizontally, and occupying about two-thirds of the space vertically. Below the orange in smaller green text was the product description: "100% Pure & Natural Orange Juice."

The new package design was visually different in many ways. The iconic orange with the straw was replaced by an almost-abstract image of a large vertical glass of orange juice covering most of the front face of the package and wrapping around the side. On the glass of orange juice, a large "100%" was printed in white text; below it in white text was the slightly smaller word "orange." The previous horizontal Tropicana brand name was now printed vertically on the right side of the package. It had to be read from the bottom to the top from the right edge of the carton. Finally, the traditional flat cap to open the package on top of the carton was replaced by a bulbous, orange-colored cap, resembling a small orange.[17]

Except for the basic carton shape, almost every aspect about the packaging was changed. The new package provided a more modern look. However, in the eyes of some experts, the increased use of white space and the simplified design made Tropicana look more like a private label product. From one day to the next, the Tropicana brand looked very different in the refrigerated shelf. While the striking visual differences between the original and the new package designs and brand logo changes are clear, the impact on the brand's customers and shopping behavior was not well understood.

Recall, the discussion about the three domains of loyalty among customers. Loyal customers who approached the shelves for this frequently purchased product may have simply found it difficult to locate their favorite brand. The visual connections were gone. The search for the familiar imagery challenged their cognitive domain (missing information) and it most likely created an emotional response of frustration and confusion (the affective domain). For many customers, this could in turn lead to a change in behavioral outcome: choosing another brand.

Accompanying the change in packaging was a dramatic change in advertising. The tagline of the new commercial ("Squeeze. It's a natural") was intended to have a double meaning: "squeeze" a friend or loved one and "squeeze" an orange. The creators of the ad may have overlooked the appropriateness of the intended emotional similarities for a product consumed primarily at breakfast. Placing the emotional scene with the new package design may have provided an additional disconnect for customers. Recall the comment by the customer interviewed in Orlando… "I like the taste of it, I like their ads. I like the way they package it." All of this was changed.

Learning from a tragedy

After less than two months Tropicana reversed its decision and returned the packaging to its original design to begin its recovery in the market. The brand providers recognized their fatal flaw in this tragic brand situation and apparently learned some lessons from the experience. Two years later, to compete with Coca-Cola's Simply Orange brand, they replaced their paper carton with a plastic PET (polyethylene terephthalate) bottle, representing yet another package redesign. While the shape and material of the packaging changed dramatically, the 2011 redesign retained its familiar brand elements: the Tropicana print logo and the straw sticking out of an orange.

This action enabled Tropicana to maintain an evolutionary, not revolutionary visual equity. The brand did not experience the dramatic customer backlash that it did in 2009. By 2022, with the overall orange juice category still in a moderate decline, PepsiCo's Tropicana Pure Premium fresh orange juice maintained a leading position in the market with a 29.8% market share, outpacing Coca-Cola's Simply Orange at 26.9%.[18]

When contemplating a creative redesign, particularly for a product that is largely bought by habit, certain brand elements must remain the same to retain on-shelf recognition. This does not imply that a brand's identity cannot be changed in a revolutionary way, it simply means that care must be taken to consider all elements of the customer's experience with the brand, especially for those customers who are very loyal to a brand. As quoted in *The New York Times* in an interview about the Tropicana misstep, the president of Tropicana North America indicated it was not the volume of people who complained about the new package design, but the fact that it came from their most loyal customers.[19]

> 'We underestimated the deep emotional bond they had with the original packaging,' he added. 'Those consumers are very important to us, so we responded, ... What we didn't get was the passion this very loyal small group of consumers have. That wasn't something that came out in the research.'

The article goes on to note that the explanation echoed a similar situation in 1985 by executives of the Coca-Cola Company in response to the avalanche of complaints when they replaced the original version of Coca-Cola with New Coke. The brand providers of Tropicana did not heed the lesson created by Coca-Cola some years earlier!

The Classic Tragedy of New Coke: Don't Mess with Our Loyalty

Recall the discussion from the early pages of Chapter 1 involving Coca-Cola's brand tragedy. It is not only supported by the events that occurred but Coca-Cola's own website hosted a page titled "The Story of One of the Most Memorable Marketing Blunders Ever."[20] That the managers involved in the situation and the company recognize its own fallibility not only qualifies it as a tragedy but also speaks to the importance of learning from these kinds of situations (an experience from which Tropicana managers apparently did not benefit). A brief recap of events provides insight into the backstory of New Coke, which along with the case of Tropicana's package change enable several lessons to be learned about the importance of the customer loyalty signpost.

Launched in 1982, it had become clear by 1983 that Diet Coke was a clear winner for the Coca-Cola Company.[21] It was the leading sugar-free soft drink and ranked fourth in market share after Coca-Cola, Pepsi, and 7Up. Diet Coke began in 1975 under the code name "Project Triangle" as a replacement for the successful Tab diet cola drink. Tab, launched in 1963, was a competitive response to Royal Crown Cola's Diet Rite cola drink, which developed market share to serve those customers desiring a sugar-free cola drink. The managers at the time believed that attaching the "Coke" brand name to a diet drink would enable it to compete more effectively with Diet Pepsi, which it did. Coca-Cola and PepsiCo became archrivals in the soft drink market.

In 1975, PepsiCo cleverly launched "Pepsi Challenge" in their advertising. The ads showed people preferring the taste of Pepsi over Coke. Pepsi's sales grew, but surprisingly not at the expense of Coke rather at the expense of other drinks. Nevertheless, it triggered the so-called Cola Wars and perturbed Coke's managers enough to seek ways to improve the taste of regular Coca-Cola and Diet Coke. During the eight-year process of developing Diet Coke, numerous formulations were developed and tested, not only for the sugar-free drink but also for regular Coca-Cola. The code name "Project Kansas" was given to the effort that resulted in New Coke: a formulation that was softer and sweeter than the original Coca-Cola secret formula. .

Substantial market research was undertaken to evaluate the decision of whether or not to go with the new product, especially taste-testing of the product with customers: "…not just a few sips by a few panels of consumers, but an exhaustive battery of 190,000 tests costing $4 million in all, with respondents from every age group and every region of the country."[22] The new product recipe was declared a substantial winner in taste tests against Pepsi and against the original Coca-Cola. This created the dilemma of deciding how to market the new formulation. Should there be two different brands for two different market segments or one? Near the end of 1984, the decision was taken to launch New Coke and take the original Coca-Cola product off the market. The launch press conference was set for April 23, 1985.

As soon as Pepsi learned of the launch, they responded immediately by declaring victory over Coke in the Cola Wars … by changing their formula, they were trying to be like Pepsi! The swift response of Pepsi raised enough media inquiries that it disrupted Coke's press conference and began a series of questions about why New Coke was launched. Despite the rocky start, the launch proceeded. The customer response was immediate and angry. Calls and letters came pouring in — ultimately some 400,000.[23] Customers asked why had they taken away Coca-Cola. Even Coca-Cola bottlers expressed anger, requesting that they be allowed to keep both.

Coca-Cola's key managers realized they had a serious problem that could jeopardize the brand name, and in early July 1985, less than three months after the launch press conference, they announced that the original drink would be returned as Coca-Cola Classic. On the day of the announcement, some 18,000 phone calls came into corporate hotlines with favorable responses for reviving the original Coca-Cola. New Coke was also allowed to be marketed until July 1992 when it was withdrawn from the market. One of the key managers involved in the New Coke launch decisions reflected on the situation:

> The simple fact is that all the time and money and skill poured into consumer research on the new Coca-Cola could not measure or reveal the deep and abiding emotional attachment to original Coca-Cola felt by so many people.… The passion for original Coca-Cola — and that is the word for it: passion — was something that caught us by surprise.… It is a wonderful American mystery, a lovely American enigma, and you cannot measure it any more than you can measure love, pride, or patriotism.[24]

Reckoning with Broken Customer Loyalties

The cases of Tropicana's package redesign and Coca-Cola's New Coke are not exceptions. There are other cases of actions taken by major brand providers that have challenged customer loyalties. For example, when the clothing store Gap changed its logo, customer response was quite negative, resulting in management returning to the original logo after six days, not to mention losses from the considerable investment with a creative agency.[25] These and other cases demonstrate the importance of understanding loyalty as a two-way street: loyalty to the brand by customers and loyalty to customers by the brand providers. Damage to either can lead to a breakdown that can sometimes destroy relationships that have taken years to develop and are costly to restore.

While the cognitive, affective, and behavioral dimensions of brand loyalty among customers have been studied extensively, it has been less so among brand providers. Not understanding the three major factors of a brand provider's cognitive, affective, and behavioral responses highlights the potential of ruptured loyalties that can lead to a brand tragedy. These often occur with misunderstanding the use of marketing research (cognitive), failing to study a brand's cultural associations (affective), and/or focusing actions on competitors while neglecting loyal customers (behavioral). Brand providers must contemplate that their actions are a result of their own cognitive, affective, and behavioral allocation of resources to customers, considered further with three recommendations.

Improve how to think about customers with comprehensive marketing research

On the surface, both case studies reveal that it is easy to criticize the value and contribution of marketing research to decision-making. The issue is not that marketing research has little value; what's more important is for brand providers to learn how to better use it to understand customer needs more deeply and accurately. In the case of New Coke, thousands of taste tests showed the new product was better than Pepsi and the original Coca-Cola. Unfortunately, taste only represents part of the customer's entire behavioral domain. It does not reflect what or how they think about the brand nor what it means to them in terms of their everyday life: their cultural existence. The research design was quite limited in scope.

When confronted with important challenges that require customer response, such as a new product design or a package change, broadening the research design to include a more comprehensive understanding of the customer's response on all three of their domains of response is essential. Marketing research is, and has always been, one of the few reliable ways to ascertain information about how customers think, feel, and do. A more comprehensive approach to the design, execution, analysis of data, and derivation of insights based on solid principles of the scientific method is required. Conducting marketing research on only one domain of customer loyalty puts important decisions at risk.

Improve how to feel about customers by understanding a brand's cultural associations

Developing an affective or emotional capability for a brand's customers is not easy. One approach to identify with a customer's emotions is to better understand the culture in which customers and the brand interact. Certain symbols evolve across culture over time and take on important and often deeper meanings, especially when associated with customer needs.

In the case of Tropicana, the category of oranges and orange juice was embedded in human culture for many years — culture being defined broadly as a handed-down way of life. The orange evokes a variety of meanings within and across various cultures.[26] In the US, orange juice became a popular breakfast drink during the 20th century. When Tropicana removed the orange from its package (replaced by an abstract glass of juice), it removed a valuable piece of culture from the customer's cognitive and affective domains that influenced purchase behaviors.

In the Tropicana case, the orange carried the value of the culture. With New Coke, it was not about the culture of "cola" but rather about the "brand" Coca-Cola; the brand itself had become part of the culture of America and beyond, not unlike Mickey Mouse as mentioned in Chapter 1. As described in the review of the Coca-Cola case, misunderstanding the deeper cultural value of the brand had an almost immediate negative response from customers. Douglas Holt provides an important discussion, along with case studies and methodology, about the importance of understanding the cultural dimensions of brands.[27] While there may be other tools and methods for firms to define, understand, and implement the emotions that define their brand, learning the culture of a brand is an encompassing concept to guide this thinking.

Concentrate behavior on the brand and its relation to customers

In both the Tropicana and New Coke cases, extraordinary attention was placed on competition. Both companies, Pepsi-Cola and Coca-Cola, virtually waged marketing wars to win over customer loyalties for their beverages. While competition has positive benefits for customers (e.g., innovation, greater value, and variety), when it is done at the expense of a brand's most loyal customers, the core brand becomes at risk. In both cases, the most vocal customers were described as their most loyal ones! A firm does not want to lose its most loyal customers, who often drive a disproportionate share of sales revenue and profit.

It is not easy for firms to ignore competitors and other market collaborators, but this should not be done at the expense of customers. Firms should be strategic, not reactive in their response to competitors. This means focusing on the brand's long-run competitive advantage, which in many cases means strengthening one's brand with customers via their cognitive, affective, and behavioral domains. For example, if a planned change is needed to cope with competition, avoid potential customer over-reaction through education about pending plans and intentions. Informing customers about impending changes to a brand may outweigh the desire to surprise a competitor with one's actions or reactions.

Propositions to Consider in Developing a Signpost for Ruptured Loyalties

A review of the Tropicana and Coca-Cola case studies reveals three critical problem areas indicating ruptured loyalties with customers. They are presented here as three summary propositions to define the signpost of ruptured loyalties from the perspective of brand providers:

- **Cognitive:** The weaker a firm's ability to *think* about its loyalty to customers, the greater the vulnerability to a brand tragedy. Carefully using the most up-to-date and useful marketing research methods and tools is essential to accomplish this.
- **Affective:** The weaker a firm's ability to *feel* its loyalty to customers, the greater the vulnerability to a brand tragedy. This often involves developing an understanding of the deep cultural needs and associations customers have for their brand.

- **Behavioral:** The weaker a firm's ability to *behave* loyally to customers, the greater the vulnerability to a brand tragedy. Organizations can easily become distracted by competitors and other stakeholders diverting important attention from customers.

There are of course other lessons from the two case studies presented in this chapter. These include the influence of economic conditions, the role of technology, the performance of suppliers and collaborators, and the quality of leaders and their leadership. However, as shown in both case studies, the inability of brand providers to develop mutual support and allegiance with their customers, especially their most loyal ones, creates potential vulnerabilities for the brand and its customers. Allocating resources in ways that ignore the totality of customers' needs, puts mutual brand loyalty at risk.

Underlying all three of these three important domains of a loyal relationship — cognitive, affective, and behavioral — is the important role of communication. How people (brand providers and customers) send and receive messages to each other to demonstrate support and allegiance to a brand (or not) is central to developing mutual loyalty. This is clearly important in a world of rapidly changing technologies that support the ability to rapidly send and receive incredible amounts of information that can influence brands. The potential impact of viral communication is considered in greater depth in Chapter 4.

Endnotes

1. "Cognition," *Lexico*. Oxford University Press and Dictionary.com (Accessed March 25, 2022).
2. American Marketing Association, *AMA Dictionary*. https://marketing-dictionary.org/b/brand-loyalty/ (Accessed March 25, 2022).
3. McGuire, W. J., "The Nature of Attitudes and Attitude Change," in G. Lindzey and E. Aronson (eds.), *The Handbook of Social Psychology*, 2nd Ed., Vol. 3, Reading, MA: Addison-Wesley, 1969, pp. 136–314. See also Breckler, Steven J., "Empirical Validation of Affect, Behavior, and Cognition as Distinct Components of Attitude," *Journal of Personality and Social Psychology*, 47, June 1984, 1191–1205.

4. Mothersbaugh, David L. and Del I. Hawkins, *Consumer Behavior: Building Marketing Strategy.* 14th Ed., New York: McGraw-Hill Education, 2020. See also Brakus, J. Josko, Bernd H. Schmitt, and Lia Zarantonello, "Brand Experience: What is it? How is it Measured? Does it Affect Loyalty?" *Journal of Marketing,* 73, May 2009, 52–68.
5. *"Cognitive," Lexico.* Oxford University Press and Dictionary.com (Accessed March 25, 2022).
6. "Affective," *Lexico.* Oxford University Press and Dictionary.com (Accessed March 25, 2022).
7. "Behavior," *Lexico.* Oxford University Press and Dictionary.com (Accessed March 25, 2022).
8. Reichheld, Frederick F., "One Number You Need to Grow," *Harvard Business Review,* 81, December 2003, 46–54.
9. Information about the history of Florida oranges and orange juice is based on Hamilton, Alissa A. "Fabricated Fresh: What Industry and the FDA Failed to Tell You About Processed Orange Juice," PhD dissertation, Yale University, 2006. ProQuest Dissertations Publishing, 2006, 3214214.
10. Lee, Ching, "The History of Citrus in California," *California Country Magazine*, March/April, 2010.
11. *"Drink* an Orange," *The Saturday Evening Post*, February 19, 1916, p. 76.
12. http://www.bingmagazine.co.uk/bingmagazine/Chapter_7.htm#Year_1948 (Accessed March 25, 2022).
13. https://www.tropicana.com/our-story (Accessed March 25, 2022).
14. Thomas, Mike, "The Big Squeeze: Three Major Orange Juice Producers are Putting the Pressure on to Win the Biggest Share of The OJ Market," *Orlando Sentinel*, September 25, 1988. https://www.orlandosentinel.com/news/os-xpm-1988-09-25-0070170114-story.html.
15. Hamilton, *Fabricated Fresh.*
16. Zmuda, Natalie, "Tropicana Line's Sales Plunge 20% Post-Rebranding," *AdAge*, April 2, 2009. https://adage.com/article/news/tropicana-line-s-sales-plunge-20-post-rebranding/135735.
17. For additional information on the Tropicana package design change with before-after photos, see: Marion, "What to Learn From Tropicana's Packaging Redesign Failure?" *The Branding Journal*, https://www.thebrandingjournal.com (Accessed December 6, 2022).

18. Jacobsen, Jessica, "2022 State of the Beverage Industry | Juice market remains weak." *Beverage Industry*, July 6, 2022. https://www.bevindustry.com (Accessed December 6, 2022).

19. Elliott, Stuart, "Tropicana Discovers Some Buyers are Passionate about Packaging," *New York Times*, February 22, 2009. https://www.nytimes.com/2009/02/23/business/media/23adcol.html.

20. "The Story of One of the Most Memorable Marketing Blunders Ever." https://www.coca-colacompany.com/news/the-story-of-one-of-the-most-memorable-marketing-blunders-ever (Accessed February 28, 2022).

21. Allen, Frederick, *Secret Formula*. New York: Open Road Integrated Media, 1994. Allen's book provides a comprehensive review of the Coca Cola story up to and including New Coke. See also Hartley, Robert F. *Marketing Mistakes*. 4th ed. New York: Wiley, 1989.

22. Allen, *Secret Formula*, p. 370.

23. Hays, Constance L., *The Real Thing: Truth and Power at the Coca-Cola Company*. New York: Random House, 2005, p. 121.

24. Allen, *Secret Formula*. p. 379.

25. Zmuda, Natalie, "Filling in the Gap of a Rebranding Disaster," *AdAge*, October 18, 2010. http://adage.com/article/news/branding-gap-s-logo-change-disaster/146525/. See also, Williams, Abigail, "Learning from the Gap Logo Redesign Fail," *The Branding Journal*, December 8, 2021. https://www.thebrandingjournal.com/2021/04/learnings-gap-logo-redesign-fail/.

26. Mazzoni, Cristina, *Golden Fruit: A Cultural History of Oranges in Italy*. Toronto, Canada: University of Toronto Press, 2018.

27. Holt, Douglas, *How Brands Become Icons: The Principles of Cultural Branding*. Boston, MA: Harvard Business School Press, 2004.

Chapter 4

Bruising Viral Spirals*

In David Bollier's book titled *Viral Spiral*, he described the Internet in terms of the empowerment of ordinary people[1]:

> It started with that great leap forward in human history. The Internet, which gave rise to free software in the 1980s and then the World Wide Web in the early 1990s .... People started to discover their own voices ... and their own capabilities ... and one another ....

The outcome generated what Bollier called the "viral spiral." *Viral* involves the ways in which new ideas and information can flourish rapidly among people, similar to a virus that generates an epidemic. *Spiral* refers to the continuously winding, widening, and networked curve of ideas that build from one central core to many other ideas. Bollier sees it as "an upward spiral of innovation," a very positive and constructive concept.

Many brand providers seek to create favorable viral opportunities to stimulate brand conversations in both B2C and B2B situations. Consider Volvo Truck's "Epic Split" 75-second B2B video, featuring Claude Van Damme. While Volvo Truck markets to business customers, its video received some 114 million views and over 60,000 comments on YouTube from 2013 to 2022![2] Certainly, a small portion of those views were by potential buyers of Volvo Trucks, but large numbers of people were sufficiently entertained by the video that they spoke to others about it, not to mention numerous parodies of the video. Clearly, the brand "Volvo"

---

*With Contributions from Sara Reid Fletcher.

achieved substantial awareness and reminders among current and potential B2B and B2C customers.

Of course, viral spirals can also be unfavorable. This is one in which an event or information about it is negative and leads to continuously undesirable, even destructive outcomes. When that event is about an incident or occurrence involving a brand, then the brand is vulnerable to a tragedy with its customers as well as its providers. These situations can be stressful for those involved and can lead to a brand being badly "bruised." The *bruising viral spiral* is therefore one in which a brand acquires vulnerability due to negative associations among customers and others that threaten its equity unless corrective actions are taken. Because a bruising viral spiral can emerge for any brand that is vulnerable to a communication wound, self-inflicted or otherwise, it is an important signpost to consider in managing the value of a brand to a firm and its customers.

In this chapter, the focus is on the travel and skincare markets. In the travel market, the emphasis is on how people travel and experience airlines. Among industries that receive bruising viral spirals, it stands out because of its high touch and face-to-face nature. People traveling with mobile phones enable them to capture unusual or interesting experiences and quickly share them with others. In the skincare market, competition can be fierce, which often prompts firms and their ad agencies to adopt overly provocative communications. When they do, customer response can be immediate, quickly spiral out of control, and threaten a brand's vitality.

United Airlines and its Friendly Skies

In his response to Question 41 at the Berkshire Hathaway Annual Meeting held on May 4, 2013, annual meeting, Warren Buffett commented on the airline industry, finding it very interesting, yet challenging[3]:

> Airline industry, very low incremental cost per seat, with enormous fixed costs. Temptation to sell last seat is very high, and hard to distinguish between which is the last seats and others. Labor intensive, capital intensive, largely commoditized. It has been a deathtrap for investors ....

Yet by early 2017 ignoring his own advice, he invested some $10 billion in four major US airline carriers, only to sell all of it in 2020 taking a loss from the precipitous decline in airline stock value due to the

COVID-19 virus pandemic. Clearly, his original judgment about airlines was correct — especially his comment about the temptation to sell the last seat and its implications for air travel.

On Sunday April 9, 2017, United Airlines Express Flight 3411 was scheduled to depart from Chicago's O'Hare International Airport to Louisville International Airport at 5:40 pm, Central Daylight Time (CDT). The flight did not depart until 7:21 pm CDT. By 6:30 pm, before actual departure, mobile phone video footage went viral showing airport police officers dragging a bloodied passenger off Flight 3411. Within 24 hours, some 1.5 million mostly negative mentions appeared on social media; it doubled within 48 hours.[4] The situation went global. Because of the Asian origin of the passenger, it became a leading online topic in China.[5] How did this happen and how was it managed by one of the world's largest airlines?

The Incident

The incident has been described in several news stories,[6] in major business school case studies,[7] and on United Airlines' own website. It is summarized here because it demonstrates how bruising the impact of viral spirals can be on a brand. The incident began with the sold-out Flight 3411 that was overbooked by one passenger. That passenger, who had not yet been assigned a seat was involuntarily denied boarding, which is consistent with US Department of Transportation airline regulations. The overbooked passenger was offered and accepted a seat on another flight, along with proper compensation for the inconvenience. All other booked passengers were then allowed to board the plane.

According to United Airlines' description of the situation,[8] an earlier flight to Louisville scheduled to depart at 2:55 pm was being delayed due to a maintenance issue and would most likely not depart until *after* Flight 3411. A crew of four members on this earlier flight had to be in Louisville that evening to operate a flight to Newark, New Jersey, early next morning. Following defined procedures, these four crew members were then booked on Flight 3411. This created the need to remove four additional seat-assigned passengers on the sold-out flight. With passengers already on the plane, the boarding agent requested four volunteers to deplane. They were offered as much as an $800 credit for future travel on United, plus meals and an overnight hotel stay. No one volunteered.

The boarding agent then properly implemented the involuntary denial of boarding process, involving the selection of four passengers to be removed from the plane. The passengers asked to deplane were two couples. One couple accepted the offer to deplane, as did the wife of the other couple. However, the husband of the other couple, 69 years old and of Vietnamese origin, refused the offer. He indicated he was a doctor and needed to be in Louisville the next morning to care for patients. After attempts to persuade the doctor to leave the plane failed, the United supervisor summoned security officers from the Chicago Department of Aviation.

Confronted with the passenger who did not want to deplane, the security officers forcibly removed him, injured him in the process, and dragged him out of the plane down the narrow center aisle. After deplaning, the doctor attempted to re-board the plane to regain his seat but was forcibly removed again. Bleeding from his face, the passenger lost teeth and suffered a broken nose during the struggle. He was taken to a hospital. Mobile phones captured video throughout the unfortunate incident, which began circulating on Twitter and other social media before the flight departed.

United's Bruising Viral Spiral

Video footage of the passenger being forced off United Flight 3411 went viral almost immediately. As would be the case for any airline in this situation, United came under pressure to address tough questions from its passengers, stakeholders, and the public. The first official response from United came at 12:37 am (EDT) on Monday, April 10 in an article published in the Louisville *Courier-Journal*.[9]

> Flight 3411 from Chicago to Louisville was overbooked. After our team looked for volunteers, one customer refused to leave the aircraft voluntarily and law enforcement was asked to come to the gate. We apologize for the overbook situation. Further details on the removed customer should be directed to authorities.

The time path of the emergence of this specific viral spiral is very well described in a New York Times article by Abby Ohlheiser, which reveals the reported sequence of events day-by-day and hour-by-hour.[10]

The viral mentions on social media began the very next morning after the incident. By noon, the hourly response rose to over 125,000 mentions. Over the day, some 1.5 million mentions were recorded, almost 70% of which were unfavorable.[11] The spike in mentions around noon may be associated with Oscar Munoz, then CEO of United Airlines, who provided the following apology in a Tweet at 12:27 pm (EDT) April 10, 2017[12]:

> This is an upsetting event to all of us here at United. I apologize for having to re-accommodate these customers. Our team is moving with a sense of urgency to work with the authorities and conduct our own detailed review of what happened. We are also reaching out to this passenger to talk directly to him and further address and resolve this situation.

The statement about "having to re-accommodate these customers" appeared to many observers to gloss over the gravity of the situation. Then, at 7:26 pm (EDT) April 10, 2017, the CEO sent a letter to employees about the situation. The letter found its way into public media outlets. Despite the apology, to many, it appeared in the letter that the CEO was defending United employees because they had no other course of action. This led to additional viral statements on social media and numerous unfavorable articles in traditional media.

In China, the viral response was believed to be based on the Asian origin of the doctor. It was reported that the incident attracted some 20 million readers per hour on Sina Weibo, the social media version of Twitter.[13] Then, on April 12, the US Department of Transportation indicated it would investigate the incident, followed by calls for further study of airline regulations by Congress (the US Senate Commerce, Science and Transportation Committee), the Illinois General Assembly, the Chicago City Council, and the Chicago Police Department.[14] The flames of the incident had been fanned.

Recovering From a Bruising Nosedive

Despite initial missteps, such as apologizing for "having to re-accommodate customers" and defending United employee actions, the CEO was determined to correct the situation. By April 11, two days after the incident, a communication process began in which he took full responsibility for the situation. This included his visits on national television shows and a statement from him indicating the airline would implement a variety of changes that would reduce the chances of similar situations happening in the future.

It is instructive to consider the chart in Figure 4.1, based on Google Trends data for the month of April 2017. The data reveal the level of interest in the term "United Airlines." Up to the evening of April 9, the pattern is relatively moderate with an average score of 4.4 over the nine-day period. However, on April 10, the first full day of the event, the interest jumped to a rating of 30 points. By April 11, it reached its peak score of 100, the maximum on the Google Trends scale and methodology for that term. During the time of April 9–11, the bruising viral exposures of the video and the ways in which the early communications were interpreted are most likely associated with this substantial increase in search interest.

Notably, after the CEO revised his communication approach, appeared on television, and apologized deeply for the incident, the search numbers began to decline. In Figure 4.1, they dropped daily from 100 to 72, to 42, to 25, and so on, until about April 18, after which they settled into a new average with much lower interest levels. The new daily average for the 12 days from April 19–30 was 6.8, still higher than the nine-day average of

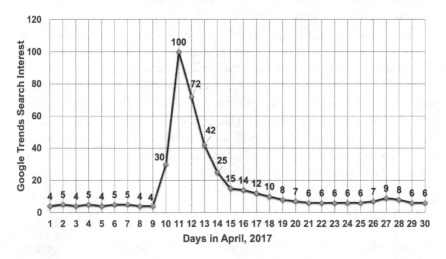

Figure 4.1.   Google Trends Search Interest for United Airlines Flight 3411, April 2017

Notes: The chart includes daily data collected from Google Trends for the month of April 2017 using the term "United Airlines." The numbers represent search interest relative to the highest point on the chart for the given region and time. A value of 100 is the peak popularity for the term. A value of 50 means that the term is half as popular. A score of 0 means there was not enough data for this term. For additional information on Google Trends and the measure, see: https://help.twitter.com/en/using-twitter/twitter-trending-faqs, (Accessed August 12, 2022).

4.4 before the incident. An important task to address for the company's marketing research would be to better understand the implications of this new slightly higher average.

By April 27, United completed its analysis of the incident and indicated 10 specific changes including actions such as limiting the use of law enforcement and customer deplaning involuntarily from seats unless safety or security is at risk.[15] United also reached a confidential resolution with the injured passenger on April 27, 2017. According to United's announcement from its website[16]:

> We are pleased to report that United and Dr. Dao have reached an amicable resolution of the unfortunate incident that occurred aboard flight 3411. We look forward to implementing the improvements we have announced, which will put our customers at the center of everything we do.

In addition, on May 12, 2017, the outcome of a Department of Transportation study of the airline's behavior in the situation was reported and did not result in a fine, nor any indication that United broke any rules nor violated the passenger's civil rights. They also concluded that United did not discriminate the passenger based on race.

United Airlines' Flight 3411 incident was not the only one by an airline that caused passengers to send messages on social media about its problems. Jet Blue Airways[17] and US Airways (acquired by American Airlines in 2015),[18] among others, have had their share of bruising media incidents.[19] However, the injurious nature of the United incident, its video recording, and the scope and extent of public response and outcry provide a valuable opportunity to better understand bruising viral spirals. Some five years after the United incident, there have been over five million views on YouTube of the event; the bruise lingers.[20]

Dove's Deep Dive

The market for skincare is large and highly competitive with almost 200 brands globally.[21] It is defined primarily by creams and lotions for the body, face, hands, and feet. It does not include cosmetics. The top 10 brands generated some 20% of total sales in 2021. The global market for skincare is valued at some $155 billion and some $21 billion in the United States. The market has grown at a rate of about 5% per year. Dove's global brand market share was some 0.5% compared to the market leader NIVEA, with 3.6%. Dove was ranked number 36 among skincare brands. However, its parent company, Unilever, was in the top five because it managed a large portfolio of skincare brands (e.g., Ponds and Vaseline). The challenge for any brand in this or any other highly competitive market is how to stand out, to be different, and to have a competitive advantage in the customer's mind.

The Dove Campaign for Real Beauty

Unilever, a British/Dutch firm and one of the largest customer products' companies in the world, developed Dove in the US in 1957 as a bar soap. Dove built its early success by highlighting the brand's functional benefits, especially that its use did not dry your skin. Advertising for the brand claimed that it was "one-quarter moisturizing cream." The brand eventually expanded to include skin care, hair care, deodorants, and personal washes.

Going into the 21st century and faced with a large growing market and the desire to improve its overall performance, Unilever declared Dove a "master brand." Among its efforts to achieve this was Dove's development and launch of the Campaign for Real Beauty. The premise for the campaign was derived from a 2004 market research study of some 3,200 customers across 10 countries. Its primary objective was to understand the extent to which women perceived and experienced themselves as beautiful.[22] A much cited finding of the research was as follows: "Only 2% of women around the world choose beautiful to describe their looks, fewer even than that choose 'attractive' (9%), 'feminine' (8%), 'good-looking' (7%) or 'cute' (7%).[23]"

However, the study also showed that of the women surveyed, some "71% are somewhat or very satisfied with their physical attractiveness and beauty." [24] Despite this potential contradiction, armed with the study, the marketing team and ad agency for Dove developed the campaign around the idea of showing real women as a counterpoint to the glamorous models often used to promote personal care products.

An initial communication to explore the possible response to the campaign idea in 2004 was a billboard showing a large attractive woman and two "tick-boxes" with the request to call a number and indicate which box was chosen. The two boxes were labeled "oversized" and "outstanding" followed by the question: "Does true beauty only fit into a size 6?" The ad struck a favorable chord with viewers. This encouraged a second more ambitious ad in 2005 for Dove's skin firming cream. It included six women of apparently different backgrounds and sizes, dressed only in white undergarments.

These initial responses encouraged Dove to expand its approach to include Super Bowl advertising and a variety of social media efforts. Dove's provocative campaign reportedly boosted sales from $2.5 billion in 2004 to $4 billion in 2014 10 years later (although a significant portion of this was also due to market growth). In 2010, Dove shifted the campaign from "Real Beauty" to "Movement for Self-Esteem," along with the theme of "Choose Beautiful." In 2013, it produced a three-minute video called "Real Beauty Sketches" that went viral on YouTube with over 69 million views in the US and 163 million views globally, winning industry communication awards in the process.[25] It represents a good example of a *positive* viral spiral for a brand provider.

In the Real Beauty Sketches video, a woman was asked to describe herself to a forensic artist. The artist, located behind a screen, would draw a portrait based on the description. A random stranger was then asked to describe the same woman to the artist during a setting. The portraits were completely different, with the one drawn based on the stranger showing a portrait of a woman who was more beautiful and attractive than the self-portrait. The campaign touched an important nerve in women about how they see themselves.

Dove's Color Vision Leads to a Bruising Viral Spiral

The success of their "beauty" and "esteem" campaigns may have emboldened Dove managers and agencies to push into zones that put their brand at risk with their customers. On Friday, October 6, 2017, Dove posted a three-second video on Facebook about its body wash products. It showed a smiling black woman taking off her top garment to reveal a white woman with a smile on her face, who then took off her top garment to reveal a smiling woman with a brownish skin color. While the video clip taken from Facebook at 11:42 am October 8, 2017 may be seen online, it may also be seen on Twitter.[26] The video set off a firestorm of reactions almost immediately.

The first responses to the ads were about its clear and visual racial bias implications. Major news outlets reported what was considered

Dove's "racist" communication. An article in the *Washington Post* summarized the viral messages and questioned Dove's motives[27]:

> Was Dove saying that inside every black woman is a smiling, redheaded white woman? Was Dove invoking the centuries-old stereotype that black is dirty and white is pure? Or that black skin can or should be cleansed away? And perhaps the biggest question of all: Did Dove really believe that the ad would make more people of color want to buy its products?

The video conjured up postings of historic ads, such as Cook's "Lightning" Soap in which a white maid scrubs a black child's face to a lighter color. Dove's apologetic response to the video was a statement on Twitter posted at 2:27 PM on October 7, 2017, just over 24 hours from the initial posting of the video: "An image we recently posted on Facebook missed the mark in representing women of color thoughtfully. We deeply regret the offense it caused."

In 2017, Dove was certainly aware of racial imagery, but their motives to use it to promote a body wash in a short video were almost certain to raise customer response. Furthermore, the video also stimulated conversation in a variety of news outlets about the possibility that Dove was capitalizing on the uncertainty in women about their looks.[28]

> Brands like Dove and Pantene have made millions by preying on women's insecurities and convincing them they need to buy products to meet societal standards of beauty …. Ads like this also reinforce the stereotype that attractiveness is the core component to determining a woman's worth.

Was Dove exploiting feminism, racial imagery, and other social issues to promote its brands, or were they truly trying to engage customers in to better meet their needs?

That Dove's parent company Unilever also marketed a brand called "Fair & Lovely" in India, a cream for skin lightening, adds even more uncertainty to their motives. On June 25, 2020, Unilever announced it would change the name of Fair & Lovely to Glow & Lovely in India. The response was an immediate firestorm on social media, especially from India. Critics accused Unilever of making only "a cosmetic change for a product that promotes harmful beauty standards."[29] Unilever defended its position. It should be noted that other companies manufacture similar products. Skin lightening is a large market globally, primarily in certain countries. While Unilever changed its brand name, Johnson and Johnson completely discontinued its Neutrogena Fine Fairness brand in response to the situation.

Are Bruising Viral Spirals Intentional?

Ultimately, one must ask the question is Dove, and perhaps other brands with similar motivations, strategically provoking current and potential customers with challenging communications intending to create a bruising viral spiral or are these simply rogue actions by managers and agency people? Was their decision to use the racially sensitive ad a tragic flaw in their brand communication or business as usual? Is there an implicit assumption that any communication bad or good enhances awareness that keeps one's brand top-of-mind among customers? Dove's brief three-second video that appeared for a short time on Facebook certainly generated a bruising viral spiral. But Dove is no stranger to controversy or racist implications.

In 2011, it generated negative customer responses from its "Before-After" body wash ad. In the ad, three women are shown going from black to brown to white, as well as in apparent reductions in body weight. Despite criticism, the company defended its brand, although its response included the following statement: "We do not condone any activity or imagery that intentionally insults any audience."[30] In 2014, Dove launched a video that showed women who wore a "revolutionary" RB-X beauty patch for 10 days felt more beautiful at the end of the 10 days than from the start of using the patch.[31] The patch was fake, a placebo with no medication. Dove's intention was to show women that they are actually more beautiful than they think. The video drew 4.5 million views on YouTube in two days. While considered successful in terms of drawing viewership, there were criticisms in the media for using deception.

It is reasonable to conclude that Dove's communication behavior with customers over the years has been intentional with an objective to generate viral spirals for its brand and for customers. However, the use of race, deception, and playing on sensitive social and psychological themes calls into question the ethics and integrity of Dove's behavior. More specifically, is Dove intentionally being provocative by generating bruising viral messages for which they can immediately apologize and that they know will heal over time? And are they doing this to stimulate customer response to keep its brand top-of-mind and enhance sales, or is it genuinely concerned about customers and their well-being? It is possible that a brand can do both, but it is worth noting that Dove's market share declined from 0.6% to 0.5% from 2018 to 2019 in a market growing at 5% annually. It may be a provocative brand strategy but not necessarily one of growth.

Propositions to Consider in Developing a Signpost for Bruising Viral Spirals

At the root of viral spirals, whether positive or negative, is the human need to share information with others. In the case of United Flight 3411, information was rapidly shared about a tragic situation experienced by a passenger. In the case of Dove, it used its provocative beauty campaign to generate emotions that motivated people to share them. Whether accidental or intentional, they stimulated controversy. In any case, once triggered, responses to a bruising viral spiral can be contagious, as in an epidemic. Three key factors can help develop and manage a signpost to anticipate and possibly ameliorate a bruising viral spiral before and after it goes out of control. These include *viral market dynamics*, *viral response planning*, and *viral engagement*.

Understand Viral Market Dynamics

Not all markets are the same, especially when it comes to the dynamic role of information and connectivity among major stakeholders. The greater the digital connectivity and related communication message dimensions of a market among customers and various stakeholders, the greater the opportunity for viral spirals to emerge. The key question that differentiates the dynamics of markets is what drives the volume and kinds of messages when substantial connectivity is available.

The viral aspects of communication are based on epidemiology and are well documented by Everett Rogers in his book on the *Diffusion of Innovations*. Rogers defined diffusion as "the process in which an innovation is communicated through certain channels over time among the members of a social system."[32] While Rogers focused on communication messages about something new (an innovation), his work laid conceptual foundations for other kinds of messages as well.

In a comprehensive review article and in his book *Contagious*, Jonah Berger focuses on word-of-mouth communication and offers several explanations why people communicate messages to others contagiously. He defines contagiousness as the likelihood that communication content can spread, similar to the way in which a virus spreads, and offers several explanations for this behavior. Briefly noted here, these explanations provide a basis for understanding the market dynamic dimensions of a viral spiral:[33]

- **Impression management:** People share messages to shape the impressions others have of them and they have of themselves. The more likely a brand's market dynamic enables impression management, the greater the likelihood of a viral spiral.
- **Emotion regulation:** Sharing messages helps people manage their emotions, when they occur, and how they experience and express them; the more likely a brand's market dynamic contains emotional dimensions (e.g., skin care), the greater the likelihood of a viral spiral.
- **Information acquisition:** Sharing messages can enable people to obtain information that reduces uncertainty by obtaining advice and solving problems. The more likely a brand's market dynamic provides useful information to customers, the greater the likelihood of a viral spiral.
- **Social bonding:** Sharing messages that bond people to others via reinforcing shared views and reducing loneliness and social exclusion. The more likely a brand's market dynamic contains information to enhance social bonding, the greater the likelihood of a viral spiral.
- **Persuading others:** Sharing messages that are emotionally polarizing and/or arousing in nature. The more likely a brand's market dynamic contains polarizing emotional messages, the greater the likelihood of a viral spiral.

Given these ubiquitous motives to share information, it may not be possible to use them to completely explain why some messages go viral and others don't. However, as Berger and Milkman point out in their research, understanding these motives may help design more effective communications.[34] Their research revealed that informational content will be more likely shared with others if it induces high-arousal emotions, especially those that are negative, e.g., evoke anxiety or anger. For example, Dove certainly generated negative emotional viral responses with its use of racial images in its video. Additional research by Tellis *et al.* revealed video ads that[35]

> "... evoked positive emotions of inspiration, warmth, amusement, and excitement stimulate significantly positive social sharing ... ads that use elements of a drama, such as surprise, likable characters, and a plot, significantly affect positive uplifting emotions and induce sharing."

While additional research is needed, especially for specific brands and product types, the promise of designing favorable over unfavorable viral spirals is promising. More importantly, for the development of a useful signpost, it is critical to understand the structure of one's current market dynamics to anticipate and possibly prevent bruising viral spirals that can damage the brand. Clearly, this requires a deeper understanding of a market's customers and other stakeholders in terms of the dimensions noted above, a primary role for market research. Nevertheless, the opportunities for a brand to experience bruising viral spirals will continue to grow with the continuously increasing ubiquity of digital connectivity. Understanding these viral market dynamics is the first requirement to build a useful bruising viral spiral signpost.

Implement Viral Response Planning

Viral response planning is about being prepared. It involves developing and implementing a *viral contingency planning process* to drive actions that *anticipate, diagnose*, and *remediate* bruising spirals.

- **Anticipate a bruising viral spiral:** This process involves far more activity than space allows here. It requires an organization to develop a sensing capability based on mapping past and potential future viral incidents with customers involving one's own brand and those of others. Uncovering additional case studies, such as described in this chapter, specific to one's markets would be most helpful. For example, in the case of United Airlines, there have been previous bruising viral spirals. In July 2008, United Airlines baggage operators roughly handled a passenger's guitar, requiring it to be repaired. The passenger, a musician, could not get a satisfactory response from the airlines to his request after nine months, so he recorded a song titled "United Breaks Guitars" and published it on YouTube on July 6, 2009.[36] The song parodied the way his guitar was mishandled and went viral on YouTube becoming one of the most popular videos at the time with some 1.6 million views. By March 1, 2023, it had over 22 million views! Anticipatory mapping processes involve studying the incident, the source from which it emerged, the timeline, signposts telegraphing key outcomes, how the incident was managed, and the outcome. The use of root-cause analysis, fishbone diagrams, design-thinking, and related methods and tools enable the development of various options to better prepare and train employees to defuse incidents that may arise. Also, the use of scenario planning and "war room" simulations can be most helpful in preparing for a difficult situation. Imagine possible bruising spirals for your brand and then cycle through the actions that could be taken.

- **Diagnose a bruising viral spiral:** Diagnosis involves studying a situation to identify symptoms and underlying causes. However, viral communications can happen with high velocity and volume and need to be detected early. For example, Herhausen *et al.* propose an ongoing detection system to track what customers are saying about the brand.[37] They suggest using text mining software along with a vocabulary of terms to identify messages about one's brand that enables managers to evaluate the level of emotional arousal. The more negative the emotional arousal, the more likely it is to go into a viral spiral. It is also possible to consider artificial intelligence, including Bayesian probability approaches, to develop customer response possibilities. For example, given input about key parameters in a specific incident, possible courses of action can be proposed, including a "most-likely" recommendation. Developing such approaches may be time consuming and costly but perhaps a minimal investment relative to the cost of a damaged brand with customers.

- **Remediate a bruising viral spiral with defined actions:** Once a bruising message is identified, brand providers need to implement a rapid response action plan to remedy the situation. For example, if a highly negative situation emerges, an up-front apology may be recommended. Non-response or delayed responses are generally unacceptable, as was the case in the United Flight 3411 incident. However, the CEO eventually followed up with an apology and subsequent actions to ameliorate the situation to some extent. While there are numerous ways to prevent different viral spirals from getting out of hand, careful planning and preparation for them are paramount.[38] All employees who may engage customers or others about a potential bruising viral spiral need to be trained and prepared to act swiftly and effectively.

While these recommendations are somewhat basic and limited, they outline a general process that providers of brands need to consider. Moe and Schweidel propose a more detailed consideration of the development and impact of "social media intelligence" on business.[39] Consider the advice of Scott Cook, cofounder of Intuit: In this age of social media in which messages can be sent and received anytime, anywhere: "A brand is no longer what we tell the consumer it is — it is what consumers tell each other it is." Bruising viral spirals can have drastic and long-lasting effects on a brand's value if not managed properly.

Execute Viral Engagement

If the dynamics of a market structure indicate the likelihood of a bruising viral spiral (positive or negative), following a response plan that indicates when and how to act and engage customers and other stakeholders is critical. Most importantly, a firm's employees and customers must clearly understand the basic rules of engagement defining the exchange process between the brand and its customers. This should occur on the first day of a brand's existence. Without these rules about how to think and respond to a potentially viral situation, misunderstandings can easily occur and can generate and intensify a bruising viral communication.

In the case of airlines, the US Department of Transportation allows overbooking. This can help every flight to leave the gate fully booked. When one or more seats are empty, the airline loses revenue it cannot replace (recall Warren Buffet's concern for investing in airlines!). Unless employees and customers understand the basic rules of engagement, the airline (or any brand provider) and its employees can make decisions that appear to be rational at one level yet trigger unintended viral consequences at another level. Upon booking, passengers need to know explicitly what happens if they are asked to leave the plane once boarded, voluntarily and involuntarily. Informing customers helps develop a cognitive understanding of a transaction that can better inform their emotional and behavioral responses. The same applies for any employees who interact with customers.

In the case of Dove, it is not known if the controversial communications involving race were created by rogue members of an agency or Dove product managers, but they should understand there are topics to which customers may respond negatively; Dove needed to educate its employees accordingly. Beyond United and Dove, any firm that operates in markets with dynamics that are prone to viral communications should educate all parties involved about how to respond to potentially difficult situations, especially regarding direct interaction with customers.

Summary: Three Propositions for Developing a Bruising Viral Spiral Signpost

Being in a market that is identified as one with a high likelihood of viral responses to occur, brand providers need a signpost that enables them to identify earlier and better those that can turn negative to avoid a brand tragedy. Three factors are considered here to use in developing a signpost for bruising viral spirals:

- **Viral Market Dynamics:** The greater the viral dynamics in a market, the greater the vulnerability to a brand tragedy.
- **Viral Response Planning:** The weaker a brand provider's viral response planning, the greater the vulnerability to a brand tragedy.
- **Viral Engagement:** The less prepared brand providers (and customers) are to engage virally, the greater the vulnerability to a brand tragedy.

While it is possible to anticipate viral communications derived from a market, it is much more difficult to anticipate and experience catastrophes that may occur. These catastrophes can arrive from sources external to a market or they can be the consequence of sources internal to a market — either from brand providers or their customers. In Chapter 5, the impact of catastrophes as a source of brand tragedies and how to cope with them are considered.

Endnotes

1. Bollier, David, *Viral Spiral*. New York: W. W. Norton & Company, Inc., 2008.
2. See: Chai, Barbara, "How Volvo Created the Jean-Claude Van Damme 'Epic Split' Video," *Wall Street Journal*, November 15, 2013;

see also: https://www.youtube.com/watch?v=M7FIvfx5J10 (Accessed June 30, 2020).

3. *Berkshire Hathaway Annual Meeting 2013*, Q41, May 4, 2013. https://www.safalniveshak.com/wp-content/uploads/2013/05/Berkshire_Hathaway_Annual_Meeting_2013.pdf (Accessed June 3, 2020).

4. Gemma, Joyce, "United Airlines Mentions Exceed 1.5 Million in a Day as Passenger Dragged From Plane," *Brandwatch*, April 11, 2017. https://www.brandwatch.com/blog/react-united-airlines-overbooked/ (Accessed December 9, 2022).

5. Waldmeir, Patti and Shannon Bond, "United Pays Heavy Price for Customer Carelessness," *Financial Times*, April 14, 2017, https://www.ft.com/content/e752feec-20f3-11e7-a454-ab04428977f9 (Accessed June 14, 2020).

6. See for example: Carey, Susan and Doug Cameron, United CEO Apologizes to Passenger Pulled From Plane, *Wall Street Journal*, April 11, 2017. https://www.wsj.com/articles/united-ceo-under-fire-for-crisis-response-says-passenger-was-belligerent-1491921299 (Accessed June 14, 2020); Wu, Tim, "How United Turned the Friendly Skies Into a Flying Hellscape," *Wired*, April 13, 2017. https://www.wired.com/2017/04/uniteds-greed-turned-friendly-skies-flying-hellscape/ (Accessed June 14, 2020); Creswell, Julie, and Sapna Maheshwari, "Dragging of Passenger Sets Off a Crisis at United," *New York Times*, April 12, 2017, Page A1.

7. See for example: Edelman, Benjamin and Jenny Sanford, "David Dao on United Airlines," HBS 9-917-026, Boston: Harvard Business School Publishing, 2017.

8. For a reprint of the United Airline's description of the situation, see: Salzberg, Barry, "United Flight 3411: What Went Wrong?" in *CU-217, Columbia Caseworks*. New York: Columbia University, 2017.

9. Aulbach, Lucas, "Video Shows Man Forcibly Removed from United Flight from Chicago to Louisville," *The Courier-Journal*, 12:17 am (EDT), April 10, 2017. https://www.courier-journal.com/story/news/2017/04/10/video-shows-man-forcibly-removed-united-flight-chicago-louisville/100274374/ (Accessed June 15, 2020).

10. Ohlheiser, Abby, "The Full Timeline of How Social Media Turned United Into the Biggest Story in the Country," April 11, 2017 at 3:31 p.m., EDT. https://www.washingtonpost.com/news/the-intersect/wp/2017/04/11/the-full-timeline-of-how-social-media-turned-

united-into-the-biggest-story-in-the-country/ (Accessed August 12, 2022).

11. Gemma, *Op. cit.*
12. Ohlheiser, *Op. cit.*
13. Minter, Adam, "Why United Likely Won't Lose Altitude in China," *Chicago Tribune*, April 12, 2017. https://www.chicagotribune.com/opinion/commentary/ct-united-airlines-angers-china-20170412-story.html (Accessed June 15, 2020).
14. Wikipedia contributors, "United Express Flight 3411 Incident," *Wikipedia, The Free Encyclopedia.* https://en.wikipedia.org/w/index.php?title=United_Express_Flight_3411_incident&oldid=960518973 (Accessed June 15, 2020).
15. For the complete list of 10 changes see: "United Airlines Announces Changes to Improve Customer Experience," *United Hub*, April 27, 2017. https://hub.united.com/search/?q=flight+3411+&searchfor=newsroom (Accessed June 16, 2020).
16. "Statement from United Airlines Regarding Resolution with Dr. David Dao," *United Hub*, April 27, 2017. https://hub.united.com/search/?q=flight+3411&searchfor=newsroom (Accessed June 15, 2020).
17. Bailey, Jeff, "JetBlue's C.E.O. is 'Mortified' After Fliers are Stranded," *New York Times*, February 19, 2007. https://www.nytimes.com/2007/02/19/business/19jetblue.html (Accessed June 19, 2020).
18. Barillas, Amanda G., "US Airways Learns a Lesson in Social Media Monitoring," *Big Fish Communications*, November 21, 2014. https://bigfishpr.com/us-airways-learns-a-lesson-in-social-media-monitoring/ (Accessed June 19, 2020).
19. Bachman, Justin, "These Airlines Fear Your Twitter Rampage the Most," *Bloomberg.com*, January 9, 2018. www.bloomberg.com/news/articles/2018-01-09/these-airlines-listen-when-you-vent-on-twitter (Accessed June 16, 2020).
20. See https://www.youtube.com/watch?v=VrDWY6C1178 (Accessed May 17, 2022).
21. The data reported in this paragraph were obtained from the source: © Euromonitor International (Accessed via Georgetown University Library on May 4, 2022).
22. Etcoff, Nancy, Susie Orbach, Jennifer Scott, and Heidi D'Agostino, "The Real Truth About Beauty: A Global Report," September, 2004. http://www.clubofamsterdam.com/contentarticles/52%20Beauty/dove_white_paper_final.pdf (Accessed June 20, 2020).

23. *Ibid.*, p. 9.
24. *Ibid.*, p. 20.
25. "Real Beauty Shines Through: Dove Wins Titanium Grand Prix, 163 Million Views on YouTube" ThinkWithGoogle.com. https://www.thinkwithgoogle.com/marketing-resources/dove-real-beauty-sketches/ (Accessed June 27, 2020).
26. The Dove video has been available on Twitter at: https://twitter.com/HasdiBravo/status/917052478738305024 (Accessed December 10, 2022).
27. Wootson, Cleve R. Jr., "A Dove Ad Showed a Black Woman Turning Herself White. The Backlash is Growing," *Washington Post*, October 9, 2017. https://www.washingtonpost.com/news/business/wp/2017/10/08/dove-ad-that-shows-a-black-woman-turning-herself-white-sparks-consumer-backlash/ (Accessed June 28, 2020).
28. Roy, Jessica, "Dear Beauty Brands: Stop Using Feminism as Your Marketing Strategy," *Time*, December 10, 2013. https://newsfeed.time.com/2013/12/10/dear-brands-stop-using-feminism-as-your-marketing-strategy/ (Accessed June 28, 2020).
29. McEvoy, Jemima, "Critics Slam Unilever Rebrand of 'Fair & Lovely' Skin Lightener as 'Glow & Lovely,'" *Forbes*, July 2, 2020. https://www.forbes.com/sites/jemimamcevoy/2020/07/02/critics-slam-unilever-rebrand-of-fair--lovely-skin-lightener-as-glow--lovely/#1558dd124b7a (Accessed July 2, 2020).
30. "Dove Body Wash Ad Stirs Controversy," *NBC*, May 26, 2011. https://www.today.com/style/dove-body-wash-ad-stirs-controversy-flna1c8368826 (Accessed April 4, 2023).
31. Neff, Jack, "Dove's 'Real Beauty' Hits a Rough Patch," *Advertising Age*, April 14, 2014.
32. Rogers, Everett, *Diffusion of Innovations*. 5th ed., New York: Free Press, 2003.
33. See: Berger, Jonah, *Contagious*. New York: Simon and Shuster, 2014 and Berger, Jonah, "Word of Mouth and Interpersonal Communication," *Journal of Consumer Psychology*, 24(4), October 2014, 586–607.
34. Berger, Jonah and Milkman, Katherine L., "What Makes Online Content Viral?" *Journal of Marketing*, 49(2), 2012, 192–205.
35. Tellis, Gerard J., *et al.*, "What Drives Virality (Sharing) of Online Digital Content? The Critical Role of Information, Emotion, and Brand Prominence," *Journal of Marketing*, 83(4), 2019, 1–20.

36. Deighton, John and Leora Kornfeld, *United Breaks Guitars* HBS 9-510-057, Boston: Harvard Business School Publishing, 2010.
37. Herhausen, Dennis, *et al.* "Detecting, Preventing, and Mitigating Online Firestorms in Brand Communities," *Journal of Marketing*, 83(3), 2019, 1–21.
38. Gregoire, Yany, Audrey Salle, and Thomas M. Tripp, "Managing Social Media Crises With Your Customers: The Good, the Bad, and the Ugly," *Business Horizons*, 58, 2015, 173–182.
39. Moe, Wendy and David A. Schweidel. *Social Media Intelligence.* Cambridge: Cambridge University Press, 2014.

Chapter 5

Catastrophes[*]

A catastrophe is defined as "an event causing great and often sudden damage or suffering: a disaster."[1] The COVID-19 pandemic virus that intensified in early 2020 certainly qualified as a disaster with catastrophic results, not only for human life but also for organizations and their survival. Over six million deaths globally were reported in the first two years after the virus was identified.[2] The impact on providers and customers of brands was also felt, but in different ways due to changing patterns of customer behavior. The Federal Reserve Bank of Boston reported that the overall number of business bankruptcy filings did not increase through the pandemic years of 2020 and most of 2021, most likely due to government support. Nevertheless, they did note that "bankruptcies were generally skewed towards very small companies, particularly for retail and restaurants."[3]

In the world of brands, the sad truth about some catastrophes is that one brand's demise can be another's gain. Industries during the COVID-19 pandemic that initially benefited were those that enabled people to remain at home yet be sufficiently connected to various sources of goods and services. These included online retailers with home delivery and providers of video communication, streaming entertainment, home fitness equipment, and food delivery services. In effect, customers of a brand that experience a catastrophe will do their best to meet their needs with other

---

* With Contributions from Daniella Arias.

options. The downside is what happens to these brands when the catastrophe ends.

Consider the case of Peloton Interactive, Inc. founded in 2012. The firm offered exercise equipment (e.g., stationary bicycles and treadmills) and monthly subscriptions to exercise classes and other connected content to motivate customer exercise experiences. The company grew steadily and went public on September 27, 2019, closing at $25 per share. By January 13, 2021, one year into the pandemic, the stock price rose to some $167, accompanied by substantial growth in customers and revenue. This corresponded to the pandemic behaviors of people spending more time at home to exercise rather than going to a gym. Unfortunately, as shown in Figure 5.1, by September 30, 2022, just three years after going public, the good fortunes of the stock price declined to about $7 per share.

Although several factors may have contributed to Peloton's precipitous decline in shareholder value (e.g., a major product recall and substantial manufacturing investments for future growth), the changing course of the pandemic to less life-threatening COVID-19 variants moved people from home exercise back to fitness gyms.[4] The strength of the Peloton brand may enable it to recover from the decline, but it will require very thoughtful strategic moves to capitalize on the umbrella of brand equity it built among its customers. As Figure 5.1 shows, the benefit of the pandemic catastrophe clearly had an upside in this case but also a downside.

In terms of brand tragedies, a catastrophe can be among the worst of those considered in this book. The swiftness, unpredictability, scale, and in some cases, the viciousness of the catastrophe can make brand recovery extremely difficult. Among the notable catastrophes that have created problems for brands and their customers was the poisonous cloud of methyl isocyanate gas that descended on Bhopal, India on the evening of December 3, 1984.[5] Although estimates vary, as many as 16,000 people may have died and more than a half million people injured by it in some way.[6] The gas emanated from a leak in the pesticide plant owned 51% by Union Carbide India Limited (UCIL) and 49% by Union Carbide Corporation (UCC). Controversy exists over the cause; UCIL claims it was improper maintenance and UCC claims it was sabotage.[7] The Supreme Court in India eventually ordered Union Carbide to pay $470 million in damages, which the company accepted.[8]

Whatever the cause of the Bhopal gas leak, the catastrophic consequences of deaths and injuries have resulted in numerous books, articles,

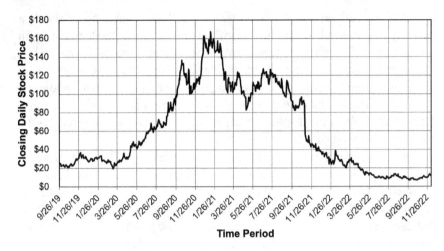

Figure 5.1.   Peloton Interactive's Pandemic Pain

Source: Based on data from https://www.nasdaq.com/market-activity/stocks/pton/historical, (Accessed December 12, 2022)

and case studies describing the incident. The apparent mismanagement of the plant during its normal operations and the mishandling of the situation after the gas leak created long-term humanitarian and legal issues for all involved. After the Bhopal disaster, Union Carbide experienced high debt obligations, which required it to sell its top consumer brands, including Prestone (antifreeze), Simoniz (car polish), Glad (trash bags), and Eveready/Energizer (batteries).

Union Carbide shrank in size through the 1990s and was ultimately purchased by Dow Chemical in 1999 as a wholly owned subsidiary.[9] A search for the Union Carbide brand on www.dow.com revealed it could not be found other than as a reference to specific manufacturing operations. Unfortunately, the Union Carbide brand and its branded products and services disappeared into the Dow world. A separate website (www.unioncarbide.com) revealed a text-based site (http://www.bhopal.com), which referenced the Bhopal catastrophe. It describes Union Carbide's presentation of the tragedy.

The Union Carbide Bhopal catastrophe is not the only one with dire consequences. In 1989, the Exxon Valdez oil tanker hit a reef off the coast of Alaska and spilled almost 11 million gallons of crude oil creating one of the world's worst environmental disasters.[10] In 1999, Merck launched Vioxx, an FDA-approved heart drug; at the same time, it launched a five-year study of its efficacy. Ineffective analysis of the data delayed the removal of the drug from the market until 2004, resulting in a reported 38,000 patient deaths from the 88,000 who took the drug.[11] These are just a few catastrophes that involve accidents, negligence, fraud, and natural disasters. In this chapter, more in-depth case studies of two brand catastrophes are presented. The learning and signposts are not derived from the catastrophe, which is often random and unpredictable, but how a brand provider responds to it.

In this chapter, two case studies are considered. The first is about Boeing, the airplane manufacturer. Its Boeing 737 MAX airplane was involved in two separate catastrophic events with complete loss of passengers and crew. How Boeing reacted to its catastrophe reveals the missteps that can occur in such an event and how to manage future crises. The second case study addresses a potential catastrophe in the "fast casual" food market. Chipotle suffered two successive outbreaks of *E. coli* and other food safety incidents that made customers ill. How the company reacted provides valuable lessons for dealing with potentially catastrophic tragedies.

Boeing 737 MAX: Airplane Tragedies

Among the worst catastrophes are airplane crashes. In its 2019 report on commercial jet airplane statistics, Boeing reported 2,030 airplane crashes between 1959 and 2018.[12] Of these, 1,398 (68.9%) were non-fatal and 632 (31.1%) were fatal. Boeing manufactured 52% of all commercial airplanes in operation by 2018. Boeing also reported that some 80% of all airplane accidents are due to pilot error versus 20% due to mechanical or maintenance error.[13] Ironically, these kinds of data may have influenced the way in which Boeing responded to two consecutive commercial airplane crashes involving its relatively new model 737 MAX airplane, which was put into commercial service on May 22, 2017.

The Boeing 737 MAX Airplane Catastrophes

The March 18, 2019 somber cover of *Bloomberg Business Week* stating "Two Planes… Five Months… 346 Dead… Boeing in Crisis" must have been painful to see for one of the leading aircraft manufacturers in the world. The first catastrophe on October 29, 2018, was Lion Air Flight 610 flying a Boeing 737 MAX out of Jakarta, Indonesia, on a domestic flight to Pangkal Pinang.[14] About a minute after takeoff, problems became apparent when the co-pilot requested altitude information, something that should have been available on the plane. Almost three minutes into the flight's climb, the plane went into a sudden 700-foot nosedive. Flight control information indicated the pilots appeared to be having difficulty controlling the plane. Some 12 minutes into the flight, the plane crashed, and all 289 people onboard died.

Almost five months later on March 10, 2019, another relatively new Boeing 737 MAX airplane took off from Addis Ababa, Ethiopia, bound for Nairobi, Kenya, on Ethiopian Airlines Flight 302. About a minute after takeoff, the control tower received a message from the crew about a flight control problem. In the next minute, the plane's flight control software system (MCAS or Maneuvering Characteristics Augmentation System) activated and sent the plane into a nosedive. The pilots recovered from the nosedive but struggled to maintain control of the aircraft. They requested a return to the airport. Then, six minutes after takeoff, the plane crashed into the ground at an estimated 600 miles per hour killing all 157 people aboard. Ethiopian Airlines grounded its Boeing 737 MAX fleet the next day.

The similarity of pilots struggling to control their respective 737 MAX airplanes prompted numerous explanations including pilot error, the plane's automated control system, and maintenance. Initially, the US Federal Aviation Administration (FAA) supported the Boeing 737 MAX after the Lion Air crash, however three days after the Ethiopian Airlines crash, the FAA decided to temporarily ground the Boeing 737 MAX aircraft. Boeing complied, grounding its worldwide fleet of 331 planes.

Airline or Airplane Manufacturer Responsibility?

After the shock of lives lost and families in mourning for their deceased loved ones, the post-airplane crash complications of blame and fault-finding amplify any such catastrophe. The root cause(s) of a tragedy influences the assignment of responsibilities that carry legal and financial implications for all involved. In addition to these concerns, airlines, leasing companies, and airplane manufacturers worry about the fears and apprehensions that an accident will have on potential travelers and their brand and model choice.

Shortly after the crash of Lion Air Flight 610, the airline was criticized, partly for its pilot training programs to support its rapid growth.

There was some concern that the Boeing 737 MAX contained a flaw that was a possible source of the problem, but it was minimal compared to the pressures placed on Lion Air. Recall, pilot error is often seen as the root cause of an airplane crash. However, Boeing's culpability in this process was by no means clear. A *Fortune* article in 2020 reported "Boeing mocked Lion Air for requesting extra 737 MAX pilot training year before crash," revealing Boeing's complicity in the potential causes related to pilot training.[15]

However, the crash of Ethiopian Airlines Boeing 737 MAX just five months later brought the airplane manufacturer clearly into the mix of responsibilities. On May 15, 2019, the *Wall Street Journal* reported the following[16]:

> In both accidents, a sensor that measures the direction of the plane's nose fed inaccurate data to the flight-control system. Reasons for the wrong data remain under investigation.

On March 9, 2020, the Ethiopian Ministry of Transport Aircraft Accident Investigation Bureau provided this initial conclusion in their Aircraft Accident Investigation Preliminary Report[17]:

> Since repetitive un-commanded aircraft nose down conditions are noticed in this preliminary investigation, it is recommended that the aircraft flight control system related to flight controllability shall be reviewed by the manufacturer.

While there may also be critics of Ethiopian Airlines pilot training and safety record, the report clearly put pressure on the FAA's decision to ground the 737 MAX. This brought Boeing's MCAS flight control software system into focus as a potential source of the airplane crashes.

Boeing's Response

A firm's responsibility in response to a major catastrophe rests with the CEO. In response to the first crash, Boeing issued a formal statement on October 29, 2018[18]:

> The Boeing Company is deeply saddened by the loss of Lion Air Flight JT 610. We extend our heartfelt sympathies to the families and loved ones of those on board.

Boeing is providing technical assistance at the request and under the direction of government authorities investigating the accident. In accordance with international protocol, all inquiries about this accident investigation must be directed to the investigating authority in charge, the National Transportation Safety Committee of Indonesia.

As one critic notes[19]:

This is a playing-it-safe, standard statement that rarely moves people to increased brand loyalty. It's overly formal and feels like a copy/paste from Boeing's crisis communications manual.... It's true that you should stick to the facts and never speculate, but when it comes to matters of the heart, tragedy and loss of life, less is not more.

Unfortunately, the initial response from Boeing and its CEO also defaulted to the "pilot error" possibility for both accidents[20]:

Muilenburg was faulted for Boeing's initial response to the accidents, when he and the company blamed the foreign pilots.

While there is no replacement for the loss of life, the criticism of Boeing and its CEO also referenced the impact on the brand[21]:

Yet investors can no longer ignore reputational risk. In today's social media-driven society, a stain on a household name like Boeing can instantly spread around the globe, piling pressure on companies and their regulators. Mr. Muilenburg initially chose to keep a low profile after the latest crash, which many investors saw as a blunder.

The CEO's personal apology came in a video 26 days after the second crash. He was replaced on December 23, 2019. After a lengthy 20-month process involving a series of hardware, software, and training changes for the planes, on November 18, 2020, the FAA signed an order to allow the 737 MAX to return to commercial service.[22] On December 29, 2020, American Airlines flew the first commercial flight with the 737 MAX from Miami, Florida to New York City.[23] Nine days later, Boeing reached a settlement with the US Justice Department:

Boeing Co. will pay $2.5 billion to resolve a Justice Department criminal investigation and admit employees deceived aviation regulators about safety issues that led to two deadly crashes of the 737 MAX, authorities said.[24]

Chipotle: Food with Integrity

Chipotle Mexican Grill was founded with a single retail outlet in 1993 by Steve Ells in Denver, Colorado.[25] The initial food offering, primarily burritos, was simple, high quality, and prepared in front of customers as they passed through a food assembly line to checkout. The founder believed in offering vegetables grown in healthy soil and meat from animals allowed to roam freely. These beliefs drove the brand's vision, mission, and strategy expressed in three words: "Food With Integrity." Customer response to the original outlet was excellent and Ells decided to expand. By 1998, Chipotle had 16 so-called "fast casual" dining outlets in Colorado. Fast casual dining is best described as food that is better in quality and taste than more traditional fast-food dining but also at a price point that is two to three times higher.

With investment from McDonald's, Chipotle was able to grow to 500 outlets by 2006. In January 2006, Chipotle undertook its initial public offering. Due to operational and other differences, McDonald's divested its interest in Chipotle during October of 2006. By August 2015, Chipotle consisted of some 2,000 company-owned outlets and its stock price was at an all-time high. But then came problems. The problems were not initially catastrophic, but they were heading in that direction. By 2016, net income dropped precipitously to $23 million from $476 million during the previous year. Concerns for food safety were attributed to the decline.

Outbreaks

Critics of Chipotle's declining performance during the last quarter of 2015 attributed it to a string of food safety issues. Managing some 54,230 hourly employees in 2,000 outlets across more than 40 states in the US, with suppliers from numerous farms and food distributors, reveals the scope of the challenges involved in serving its customers fresh meals every day.

Food safety concerns were not new to Chipotle in 2015. In March and April 2008, a hepatitis A outbreak was traced to a single restaurant in San Diego County, California, that infected 22 customers. In April 2008, some 400 customers who ate at a Chipotle in Kent, Ohio, experienced the effects of a norovirus. In February 2009, an outbreak of campylobacteria was traced to a Chipotle outlet where chicken was not adequately cooked. Fortunately, the outbreaks remained local and did not escalate beyond specific restaurants.

However, the onslaught of outbreaks beginning July 2015 drew national attention to the problem with serious impact on its performance and brand. Without going into detail for each one, consider the following list of outbreaks[26]:

- July 2015, *E. coli* outbreak (Seattle, Washington, five customers);
- August 2015, norovirus outbreak (Simi Valley, California, 98 people, 18 of whom were employees);
- August 2015, Salmonella outbreak (Minnesota, 64 people, 22 outlets);
- October 2015, *E. coli* outbreak (55 people in 11 states);
- November 2015, *E. coli* cases (five people in two states);
- December 2015, norovirus outbreak (141 people, including 80 students from Boston College, one store).

Fortunately, there were no reported deaths from these food-borne illnesses. However, the brand relationship between Chipotle and its customers was clearly at risk with concern about the troubling sequence of outbreaks — a possible catastrophe in the making.

Response to Food-borne Illness

Chipotle customers were unhappy with the continuous stream of bad news about the safety of eating at one of its outlets. This was compounded by the involvement of the United States Center for Disease Control, which conducted investigations of the various outbreaks. Negative social media comments from customers flourished on Instagram, Facebook, Twitter, and other platforms. In addition, articles published in daily and national newspapers and magazines, stories on radio and television, and articles in other media kept the issue top of mind and raised fears about the continuing safety of food quality at Chipotle.[27] Customer visits and sales declined.

The response from management to the initial 2015 outbreaks was highly local. That is, each problem was treated separately. For example, in the October 2015 outbreak of *E. coli*, it was reported that the company closed 43 stores in the States of Oregon and Washington to clean each store and identify the source of the virus. The company also worked with health officials to identify the sources of the problems. This was a pattern followed in almost every outbreak. While some considered these initial responses from top management to be minimal, by the time of the Boston outbreak in late November and early December, they could no longer be treated as local; it had become a national issue.

Pathogens and sources of the outbreaks were sufficiently different such that the focus of concern evolved around the company's principles and practices. In recognition of these growing concerns, on December 10, 2015, Mr. Ells went on *NBC*'s nationally televised *Today Show* to apologize to Chipotle customers about food safety. This was followed by an official letter of apology published in a full-page advertisement in 61 major newspapers around the country, along with a series of promised improvements[28]:

> The fact that anyone has become ill eating at Chipotle is completely unacceptable to me and I am deeply sorry. As a result, we are committed to becoming known as the leader in food safety, just as we are known for using the very best ingredients in a fast-food setting.

While some considered the initial response from top management to be minimal, the Chipotle Annual Report published in February 2016 did not hide from seriously addressing the food safety challenges it faced during the last half of 2015. It revealed the deeper concerns of Steve Ells and the management team for its customers and the perception of its brand.[29]

> We believe the impact of these incidents on our sales has been exacerbated in part by the high expectations many customers have for us as a result of our Food With Integrity mission, and our failure to meet those expectations may make recovery more difficult for us. Additionally, the significant amount of media coverage regarding these incidents and the impact of social media (which was not in existence during many past food safety incidents involving other restaurant chains) in increasing the awareness of these incidents may also negatively impact our ability to recover from these incidents.

Regaining the Customer's Appetite

The food safety incidents put Chipotle in a double bind of sorts. It built its success on "Food With Integrity," yet the very problems faced were the unpredictable risks of food (and food handling) *without* integrity. To correct the situation, Mr. Ells and the management team took several key steps. They developed an improved food safety system, retrained employees, dealt quickly and fairly with legal cases, and improved their marketing.

Chipotle hired a food safety expert to devise an aggressive food safety process that not only would check existing outlets but also create a rapid response system for any specific outbreaks.[30] To design a system that instilled safety at every step of the process eventually required a more centralized approach to growing, harvesting, transporting, and storing ingredients. For example, larger farms were used that could afford the technology to scan for pathogens in their produce. Produce that passes the tests would then be shipped to commercial kitchens for further testing and processing before going to the restaurants. To illustrate, rather than cutting tomatoes fresh by hand in each outlet, this core ingredient would arrive pre-cut in plastic containers.

In addition to a new food safety system, on February 8, 2016, Chipotle closed all its stores for a few hours to explain to employees their response to the food safety incidents.[31] This involved explaining new safety measures, as well as allowing employees to ask questions. This was part of a new program retraining employees in food handling, hygiene (e.g., hand washing and plastic gloves), and provisions for paid sickness benefits — pending nurse approval, sick employees should not come into the restaurant to work, but they would get paid. This was a consequence of issues with employee hygiene, cited in some of the food safety outbreaks.

Despite these efforts, in 2017, an ill food handler at a restaurant in Sterling, Virginia, was the likely source of norovirus that reportedly sickened some 135 people. Another 647 people were sickened in a July 26–30, 2018 outbreak of clostridium perfringens at a Chipotle in Powell, Ohio. Clostridium perfringens, an infectious bacterium, is often caused by warmed meat that is allowed to cool before refrigerating. Using its rapid response food safety system, it closed the store on July 30, thoroughly cleaned the restaurant, and replaced all the food for a reopening the next day.[32]

Chipotle also experienced numerous legal cases as a result of its food safety issues, however its approach was to settle them fairly and quickly. In April 2020, the United States Department of Justice fined Chipotle $25 million for its entire series of seven food safety outbreaks from 2015 to 2018, one of the largest in US history. Chipotle agreed to pay the fine and to "develop and follow an improved, comprehensive food safety compliance program."[33]

In responding to customers about food safety, marketing became critical to recover lost customers and ultimately grow the business again. Based on its research, Chipotle learned that its most loyal customers visited less often during the crises, especially during the last quarter of 2015 when several incidents occurred. To get them back into the restaurants, they were offered coupons, and a large proportion responded favorably. As a result, couponing became a favorite marketing tactic to bring back business.[34] However, coupons are expensive and don't always build the brand. In attempts to rebuild the brand, Chipotle's marketing agencies developed cartoon story videos that showed the values of its "Food With Integrity" mission. The firm also developed a loyalty program that rewarded returning customers.[35]

Chipotle struggled for three years to retain and maintain its customer base. Its return to growth did not begin until 2018. Under the helm of a new CEO, Chipotle began to invest more systematically in its marketing to rebuild brand relationships with its customers. It developed a digital campaign to make ordering and pickup at stores easier for its current and potential customers. In addition to launching new stores, new menu items were added, as well as catering and delivery options.[36]

From 2018 through 2019, the chain began to show improved results, largely through the growth in the number of stores (2,622 in 2019 versus 2,010 in 2015).[37] With the new CEO, new product development for menu items followed a much more systematic process than in the past. By 2019, marketing spending doubled to some $140 million from $70 million in 2015. This investment in social media and advertising also contributed to its improved relationships with consumers about the brand: tasty "Food With Integrity," at a fair price, and served quickly.[38]

The chart of Chipotle's stock price over a 10-year period in Figure 5.2 reveals the impact of the food safety challenges. The company was launched in 2006 at a price of $20 per share and grew steadily in its stock price through the number of stores and the customers it served until 2015. As described in the preceding sections, during 2015, it began to experience numerous food safety issues, even to the point of being recognized in Chipotle's 2016 annual report. Not surprisingly, the value of the stock began to decline fairly consistently from a high of $750 a share during 2015 to a low of $270 during 2017.

Because of the aggressive and persistent actions taken by management to remediate their food safety problems, they may have clearly

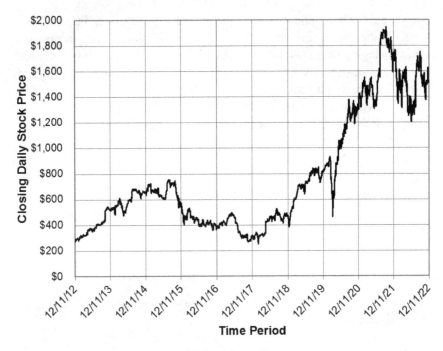

Figure 5.2. The Interrupted Rise of Chipotle's Stock

Source: Based on data from https://www.nasdaq.com/market-activity/stocks/cmg/historical, (Accessed December 12, 2022).

avoided a continuing decline and perhaps any truly catastrophic consequences. The confidence in Chipotle appears to have been restored, at
least as evidenced by the response of investors in its stock price as shown
in Figure 5.2. During 2021, the stock price grew to over $1,900 per share
and settled back to $1,700 per share in 2022. The firm operates more than
3,000 stores, still managing to maintain its food with integrity strategy.
Despite the success, Chipotle and other food-service brands will still need
to be vigilant about food safety and develop useful signposts to alert
operations of possible outbreaks.

Mission Impossible: Coping with Catastrophes

Every catastrophe for a brand will be different. It may come when it is
least expected, and it may carry consequences that may never be known.

Indeed, any catastrophe can become a brand's "mission impossible." Whatever the catastrophe, and despite the severity and gravity of the outcome, managing the catastrophe as effectively as possible will be required to secure a reasonably good outcome. Crisis management experts and their advice can and most likely should be obtained to assist in coping with a catastrophe. However, there are some basic signposts that are briefly summarized here to consider as one goes forward. While they are somewhat consistent with those from brand tragedies in previous chapters, they carry substantial weight due to their catastrophic nature. They include developing a well-framed response and acting immediately, analyzing the systems to solve the problems that sourced the catastrophe, and maintaining and strengthening business and marketing strategies to the extent possible.

Develop a Well-Framed Response and Act Immediately

The first response to a catastrophe will have the greatest impact on everyone. It should be

- about the people involved and not about one's organization or brand;
- done immediately after the event;
- communicated by the organization's leader.

In retrospect, it will most likely not be the precisely correct response, but the catastrophe should be "framed" to do the right thing for as many people involved as possible. In the case of Boeing, the initial comments about apologies for the loss of life were appropriate, but subsequent statements about the cause of the catastrophe triggered the undesirable "blame game."

As Sandra Sucher writes in the *Harvard Business Review*, Boeing's CEO reported to the President of the United States that the 737 MAX planes were safe, thereby shifting the blame to pilot training — an assumption that might be perfectly logical given the research data that 80% of crashes are due to pilot error. As Sucher notes in her discussion of framing: "So Muilenburg's frame appears to be: *This is a technical problem that we can correct with pilot training.*" She then goes on to propose the framing that should have been used instead:

A better frame would be: *This is a technical problem that we do not fully understand. In light of that uncertainty, we recommend grounding the 737 MAX 8s and 9s until we can be sure we know what is causing these crashes, and can satisfy ourselves and all of the global regulators that the plane is safe to fly again.*

A better framing of the situation does not assign blame but fully recognizes the uncertainty around the cause of the catastrophe, takes immediate action, and highlights the importance of the situation by including important collaborators.

Analyze the Systems to Solve the Problems that Sourced the Catastrophe

There are some catastrophes that emanate from systems that are beyond a company's control. They are the ones brought on by weather disasters, pestilence, disease, and similar sources. Those that arrive from systems that cannot be fixed should nevertheless be studied to aid in erecting barriers or other defenses against catastrophes when they occur. For example, flooding caused by unpredictable weather systems may be anticipated and partly controlled by strategically placed dams. Similarly, understanding the epidemiological path of pandemics may have cautioned Peloton to moderate its manufacturing plant investments throughout the track of COVID-19. In any case, systems that may be the source of a catastrophe require in-depth study and analysis to find and correct the source of the problem.

This was a process that Boeing was eventually required to undertake. This included not only the analysis of the MCAS flight control system but also how the sensors on the plane triggered inflight responses and the subsequent human responses. In addition, manufacturing processes, pilot training/retraining, airplane maintenance, regulatory actions, legal, and other related factors involved in the entire flight control system required deep analysis. Once the entire system and set of sub-systems were understood, a reliable set of fixes were tested and implemented as a basis to restore confidence in the 737 MAX brand.

In the case of Chipotle, what may have been on the minds of managers in deciding how to successfully manage through their food safety crisis was the 1993 "Jack in the Box" fast-food chain's *E. coli* crisis. An outbreak of *E. coli* across 73 of its restaurants in four states resulted in the deaths of four children and 732 others who became ill, many of whom experienced permanent health damage.[39] Yet Jack in the Box survived this catastrophic event. It took the better part of three years, but the company survived. Their process could have been, and perhaps was, a playbook for Chipotle's survival.[40]

A key part of the Jack in the Box survival depended on its persistence in analyzing the systems that were the sources of *E. coli* and correcting them. This included managing the risk of serving undercooked beef for its hamburgers. The solution that Jack in the Box developed from studying its food safety system evolved from the hazard analysis methodology developed by the National Aeronautics and Space Administration (NASA) in the US and ultimately became the industry standard.[41]

> The system, known as 'hazard analysis critical control points,' tracks food from the farm to the consumer by monitoring temperatures in delivery trucks and providing restaurant employees with priority check-lists for everything from scrubbing equipment to handling food.

In many ways, Chipotle followed a similar process, yielding a food safety system for delivery to its restaurants that addressed its series of problems.

Rebuild Customer Trust with Strategic Consistency and Marketing

For many catastrophes, the strategy that brought initial success should remain the focus of core business decisions to the extent possible. It is not the time to overhaul top management or change one's competitive advantage. Strategically, Boeing faced the difficulty of how to go forward with the Boeing 737 MAX, one of its best-selling airplanes and the most important product in its aircraft portfolio. It was designed as a response to a successfully updated single-aisle airplane by Airbus, its main competitor. It could not abandon the strategy.

Boeing's Board of Directors undertook a more detailed study of the serious problems, worked with the FAA, and eventually gained approval that the serious problems were resolved. Given the size of Boeing and its role as one of the two major commercial airplane manufacturers in the world, its brand will most likely survive. However, lingering issues associated with corporate responsibility, almost four years after the first crash, will require time for the company and brand to return to its former status.[42]

As Boeing goes forward with its 737 MAX, it will have to thoughtfully engage all levels of its customer base along the value chain — from potential leisure and business passengers, airlines, 3rd party booking services, and other collaborators. Active involvement to engage customers in a variety of media will provide clues not only for a strategic marketing plan but also for future brand-building communications with customers. Such a response will require its current and future business leaders to be multi-talented, not only with marketing competence but also with all aspects of the business enterprise.

In the case of Chipotle, the initial steps after improving its food safety processing relied on coupons to bring back its most loyal customers. It then decided to enter new fast-food businesses, including Asian food (ShopHouse Southeast Asian Kitchen) and hamburgers (TastyMade). By 2018, none of these were succeeding and were subsequently closed, a deviation from their core strategy. Fortunately for Chipotle, the CEO and firm did not abandon their core strategy of Food With Integrity, which could have been easy to do because it was so intensively threatened by the four-month series of food safety outbreaks. Instead, the firm responded with a new CEO and management team in 2018 that rebuilt the business through more intense marketing on its Food With Integrity strategy to better connect with its customers.

The Chipotle team eventually reinvested in marketing once it was clear that it had repaired its food safety problems. Communication prior to the system fix was minimal; the firm settled legal claims as quickly as possible and did its best to reassure Wall Street that things would eventually return to normal.[43] It took three years to fully recover from the crisis. Its marketing began when the new president brought in a new Chief Marketing Officer (CMO), who built an "agile" team of marketing people.[44] The objective was to increase customer engagement with a new marketing playbook that would focus on the quality of its food.

The first step to build engagement was going digital with its customers in terms of communication and food delivery. It then developed a new messaging approach based on the idea of "For Real," which took it back to the core value of its food and enabled it to communicate with new and potential customers. The team was opportunistic with video and other social media efforts that got more people talking about the brand. Finally, it developed a customer loyalty program that enabled it to reconnect with former customers, add new ones, and most effectively rebuild its brand with customers. Business success followed.

Propositions to Consider in Developing a Signpost for Catastrophes

On one hand, it seems implausible that a signpost for catastrophes can be developed. On the other hand, being in a market or business situation with the potential for a catastrophe compels one to consider the composition of such a signpost. The question is as follows: Can a signpost be developed for a brand provider's market that reduces the likelihood of a brand tragedy due to a catastrophe? The answer is "yes" based on the Chipotle experience, but with the caveat that it does not guarantee the amelioration of consequences of the catastrophe. Practically, it only helps brand providers prepare for one and think through a firm's readiness to cope with one. The three factors considered above to foster the development of a signpost for catastrophes are briefly summarized here as propositions:

- **Develop a Well-Framed Response:** The more difficult to frame an immediate strategic response, the greater the vulnerability to a brand tragedy.
- **Analyze the Systems Sourcing Catastrophic Problems:** The more difficult to conduct a proper systems analysis, the greater the vulnerability to a brand tragedy.
- **Rebuild Customer Trust with Marketing:** The more difficult to rebuild customer trust, the greater the vulnerability to a brand tragedy.

The challenges to respond to a major catastrophe are immense. These summary propositions are but a beginning to a more comprehensive playbook necessary to anticipate possible catastrophes and with careful thought and planning ameliorate the consequences as much as possible. The purpose of such a signpost is to encourage brand providers to anticipate possible catastrophes, prepare for them, and learn from them. As H.G. Wells has often been quoted:[45] "Human history becomes more and more a race between education and catastrophe." In any case, as will be seen in Chapter 6, the underlying key driver of response to and preparation for a catastrophe is a firm's leaders!

Endnotes

1. Oxford University Press (2020 catastrophe. In: Lexico.com. Available at: https://www.lexico.com/definition/catastrophe) (Accessed July 6, 2020).
2. Johns Hopkins University, Coronavirus Resource Center. https://coronavirus.jhu.edu (Accessed July 13, 2022).
3. Collins-Thompson, Juli, Brendan Collins, and John Maher, "Review of U.S. Business Bankruptcies During the COVID-19 Pandemic," Federal Reserve Bank of Boston, SRA Notes, issue number: 2021–05, November 19, 2021, p. 14. Their findings on the rates of bankruptcies are consistent with later reports by the United States Bankruptcy Courts, "Bankruptcy Filings Drop 24%," February 4, 2022, https://www.uscourts.gov/news/2022/02/04/bankruptcy-filings-drop-24-percent (Accessed May 14, 2022).
4. See Gregg, Aaron and Hamza Shaban, "Peloton feels the burn as Americans head back to the gym," *Washington Post*, November 5, 2021. https://www.washingtonpost.com/business/2021/11/05/peloton-sales-gym-memberships/ (Accessed May 15, 2021) and Terlep, Sharon, "This Half-Built Ohio Factory Shows How Peloton Mismanaged the Pandemic," *Wall Street Journal*, May 21, 2022, https://www.wsj.com/articles/this-half-built-ohio-factory-shows-how-peloton-mismanaged-the-pandemic-11653105627?mod=hp_lead_pos7 (Accessed May 21, 2022).
5. Diamond, Stuart, "The Bhopal Disaster: How It Happened," *New York Times*, January 28, 1985, https://www.nytimes.com/1985/01/28/world/the-bhopal-disaster-how-it-happened.html.
6. Eckerman, Ingrid, *The Bhopal Saga — Causes and Consequences of the World's Largest Industrial Disaster.* India: Universities Press, 2005.
7. See Union Carbide's website for their report on the disaster, http://www.bhopal.com (Accessed July 5, 2020).
8. Hazarika, Sanjoy, "Bhopal Payments By Union Carbide Set At $470 Million," *New York Times*, February 15, 1989. https://www.nytimes.com/1989/02/15/business/bhopal-payments-by-union-carbide-set-at-470-million.html (Accessed July 5, 2020).
9. Warren, Susan, "Dow Chemical to Acquire Union Carbide — Deal, Valued at $8.89 Billion, Would Position Firm to Challenge DuPont," *The Wall Street Journal*, August 5, 1999. https://www.wsj.com/articles/SB933766485647859030 (Accessed July 6, 2020).

10. Wikipedia contributors, "Exxon Valdez oil spill," Wikipedia, The Free Encyclopedia, https://en.wikipedia.org/w/index.php?title= Exxon_Valdez_oil_spill&oldid=965193826 (Accessed July 5, 2020).
11. Prakash, Snigdha and Vikki Valentine, "Timeline: The Rise and Fall of Vioxx," NPR November 10, 2007. https://www.npr.org/2007/11/10/ 5470430/timeline-the-rise-and-fall-of-vioxx (Accessed July 5, 2020).
12. *Statistical Summary of Commercial Jet Airplane Accidents, Worldwide Operations*, 1959–2018, 50th ed., Chicago: Boeing Corporation, September 2019. http://www.boeing.com/resources/boeingdotcom/ company/about_bca/pdf/statsum.pdf (Accessed July 12, 2020).
13. Rankin, William, "MEDA Investigation Process," *Boeing Aero Quarterly*, Quarter 2, 2007, pp. 15–21 (Accessed July 12, 2020).
14. The description of the two Boeing Max 737 airplane crashes in this section are based on the following source: Chappell, Bill and Laurel Wamsley, "FAA Grounds Boeing 737 MAX Planes in U.S., Pending Investigation," NPR Business, March 13, 2019; Langewiesche, William, "What Really Brought Down the Boeing 737 MAX?" *New York Times Magazine*, September 18, 2019; Wikipedia contributors, "Ethiopian Airlines Flight 302," *Wikipedia, The Free Encyclopedia*, https://en.wikipedia.org/w/index.php?title=Ethiopian_Airlines_ Flight_302&oldid=963981361 (Accessed July 12, 2020); Wikipedia contributors, "Lion Air Flight 610," *Wikipedia*, The Free Encyclopedia, https://en.wikipedia.org/w/index.php?title=Lion_Air_Flight_610& oldid=965338436 (Accessed July 12, 2020).
15. Beene, Ryan and Harry Suhartono, and *Bloomberg*, "Boeing Mocked Lion Air for Requesting Extra 737 MAX Pilot Training Year Before Crash," *Fortune*, January 14, 2020. https://fortune.com/2020/01/14/ boeing-lion-air-extra-737-max-pilot-training-simulator-crash/ (Accessed July 19, 2020).
16. "Boeing MAX: A Tale of Two Crashes," *The Wall Street Journal*, May 15, 2019. https://www.wsj.com/graphics/boeing-max-tale-of- two-crashes/?mod=article_inline (Accessed July 14, 2020).
17. "Aircraft Accident Investigation Preliminary Report," Federal Democratic Republic of Ethiopia: Ministry of Transport Aircraft Accident Investigation Bureau, Report No. AI-01/19, March 9, 2020, p. 25.
18. https://boeing.mediaroom.com/news-releases-statements?item= 130327 (Accessed July 15, 2020).

19. DeLay, Melissa, "Boeing: What NOT to Do When Crisis Hits Your Company," *True Perception*, May 2, 2019. https://truperception.com/boeing-what-not-to-do-when-crisis-hits-your-company/ (Accessed July 15, 2020).

20. "Boeing Fires Its CEO Due to 737 MAX Crashes Response," Associated Press, December 24, 2019.

21. Sindreu, Jon, "Why Boeing Needs to 'Own' the 737 MAX Debacle," *The Wall Street Journal*, April 24, 2019. https://www.wsj.com/articles/why-boeing-needs-to-own-the-737-max-debacle-11556127111 (Accessed July 19, 2020).

22. "FAA Statement on Boeing 737 MAX Return to Service," United States Department of Transportation, Federal Aviation Administration, November 18, 2020. https://www.faa.gov/news/updates/?newsId=93206 (Accessed December 27, 2020).

23. Tangel, Andrew, "Boeing's 737 MAX Returns to U.S. Commercial Service With American Airlines Flight," *Wall Street Journal*, December 29, 2020. https://www.wsj.com/articles/american-airlines-resumes-737-max-passenger-flights-11609253579?mod=searchresults_pos4&page=1 (Accessed January 5, 2021).

24. Michaels, Dave, Andrew Tangel and Andy Pasztor, "Boeing Reaches $2.5 Billion Settlement of U.S. Probe Into 737 MAX Crashes," *Wall Street Journal*, January 7, 2021. https://www.wsj.com/articles/boeing-reaches-2-5-billion-settlement-of-u-s-probe-into-737-max-crashes-11610054729 (Accessed January 14, 2021).

25. Historical aspects of the development of Chipotle and its food safety crises in this section and the next are based on this Wikipedia summary of events: Wikipedia contributors, "Chipotle Mexican Grill," *Wikipedia, The Free Encyclopedia*, https://en.wikipedia.org/w/index.php?title=Chipotle_Mexican_Grill&oldid=967651663 (Accessed July 19, 2020).

26. *Ibid.*

27. Long, Heather, "Chipotle's Reputation Gets Slammed, CNN Money," December 10, 2015. https://money.cnn.com/2015/12/10/investing/chipotle-ecoli-norovirus-reputation/index.html (Accessed July 11, 2020).

28. Harrison, Ian, "Sorry, America: Chipotle CEO Offers Fat Newspaper Ad Apology," *Eater*, December 16, 2015. https://www.eater.com/2015/12/16/10310980/chipotle-ceo-apology-steve-ells (Accessed July 11, 2020).

29. Chipotle Mexican Grill, Inc., 2016, Annual Report, p. 10. http://www. annualreports.com/Company/chipotle-mexican-grill-inc (Accessed July 9, 2020).
30. Berfield, Susan, "Inside Chipotle's Contamination Crisis," *Bloomberg Business Week*, December 22, 2015. https://www.bloomberg.com/ features/2015-chipotle-food-safety-crisis/ (Accessed July 12, 2020).
31. McCoy, Kevin and Katharine Lackey, "Chipotle to Close All Stores on February 8 for All-Staff Meeting on Food Safety," *USA Today*, January 15, 2016. https://www.usatoday.com/story/money/2016/01/15/reports-chipotle-close-stores-feb-8-food-safety-review/78841420/ (Accessed July 12, 2020).
32. "Chipotle Agrees to Pay $25 Million Federal Fine for Role in Some Outbreaks," *Food Safety News*, April 22, 2020. https://www.food safetynews.com/2020/04/chipotle-agrees-to-pay-25-million-federal-fine-for-role-in-some-outbreaks/# (Accessed July 12, 2020).
33. *Ibid.*
34. Jargon, Julie, "Chipotle Counters Frightful Results," MarketWatch, April 23, 2016. https://www.marketwatch.com/story/chipotle-counters-frightful-results-2016-04-23-10485737 (Accessed July 12, 2020).
35. Olson, Elizabeth, "After Food Safety and Drug Scandals, Chipotle Seeks a Fresh Start," *New York Times*, July 10, 2016. https://www. nytimes.com/2016/07/11/business/media/after-food-safety-and-drug-scandals-chipotle-seeks-a-fresh-start.html (Accessed July 12, 2020).
36. "Chipotle to End Fiscal Year 2018 On High Growth Great Speculations," *Forbes*, February 5, 2019. https://www.forbes.com/ sites/greatspeculations/2019/02/05/chipotle-to-end-fiscal-year-2018-on-high-growth/#6d8c964b3452 (Accessed July 12, 2020).
37. The financial statistics in this paragraph are derived from Statista Dossier, Chipotle Mexican Grill. https://www-statista-com.proxy. library.georgetown.edu/study/31640/chipotle-mexican-grill-statista-dossier/ (Accessed July 12, 2020 from Georgetown University Library).
38. Garcia, Tonya, "Chipotle's CEO Explains How His Company Achieved a Surprising Comeback That Has Sent Its Stock Rocketing," *Market Watch*, September 29, 2019. https://www.marketwatch.com/ story/chipotles-ceo-says-this-is-how-the-company-went-from-making-customers-retch-to-making-shareholders-rich-2019-09-20 (Accessed July 12, 2020).
39. Schlosser, Eric, *Fast Food Nation*. London: Penguin Books, 2001.

40. Veverka, Mark, "Marketing Savvy Helps Jack in the Box Survive," *The Wall Street Journal*, August 6, 1997. https://www.wsj.com/articles/SB870804435643828500 (Accessed July 12, 2020).
41. Veverka, *Ibid*.
42. Chokshi, Niraj, "Former Boeing Pilot is Cleared of Fraud Charges in 737 Max Case," *New York Times*, March 24, 2022, Section B, Page 3.
43. Bradley, Diana, "The Man Who Saved Jack in the Box's Brand After Its *E. Coli* Crisis Has Advice for Chipotle," *PR Week*, December 23, 2015. https://www.prweek.com/article/1377882/man-saved-jack-boxs-brand-its-e-coli-crisis-advice-chipotle (Accessed July 18, 2020).
44. Odell, Patty, "Chipotle Roars Back from Food Crisis with Hard-Hitting Strategy," ChiefMarketer.com, October 22, 2019. https://www.chiefmarketer.com/chipotle-roars-back-from-food-crisis-with-hard-hitting-strategy/ (Accessed July 18, 2020).
45. Wells, H. G., The Outline of History: Being a Plain History of Life and Mankind, London: Cassell and Company, Ltd., 1920.

Chapter 6

Leadership Lost[*]

The world has experienced excellent leadership throughout the years. Unfortunately, it has also had its share of poor leadership. Whether in business, government, social institutions, or other organizational forms, people have suffered from the intellectual, emotional, and behavioral limitations of so-called "leaders." In many profit and non-profit organizations, the primary leader or chief executive officer (CEO) is the cornerstone of its brand and how it is perceived by its customers. From previous chapters, recall the leaders of Blackberry, Coca-Cola, United Airlines, Boeing, and the central roles they played when faced with a brand tragedy.

Leaders are increasingly placed under significant scrutiny for managing their companies, defining their brands, and connecting their brand with customers. It is an unwelcome headline in a business newspaper when an article is titled: "Amazon Didn't Cripple Bed Bath & Beyond. Its Own Leaders Did.[1]" In a world of rapidly changing competitors, customers, technologies, market trends, regulatory activity, and other factors, the leaders of an organization become the focus for its brand and the ones who set the stage for an organization's agility in response.

When Congress decided to challenge the competitiveness of four major technology companies, they called the CEOs to testify. On July 29, 2020, Jeff Bezos from Amazon.com Inc., Tim Cook from Apple Inc., Mark Zuckerberg from Facebook Inc. (subsequently renamed to Meta Platforms, Inc.), and Sundar Pichai, from Google LLC appeared before members of the House Antitrust Subcommittee to answer questions

---

[*]**With contributions from Katherine Miyamasu.**

challenging their competitive activities.[2] Questions were raised about how the companies may have used their large online platforms in anti-competitive ways. They defended their positions and their brands by indicating their focus on innovation and meeting customer needs. Each one clearly understood his role in protecting the value of the brand.

In some cases, the brand becomes synonymous with its leader. Consider the case of Steve Jobs and Apple. Although his route to company leadership was lengthy, he carefully crafted the face of one of the world's most innovative brands and how it connected with customers. His development and launch of the "Think Different" campaign propelled Apple's brand into a new era of innovation. He invited everyone to join the conversation about the Apple brand. Steve Jobs' willingness to take risks with innovation and reject complacency became a hallmark of Apple.[3]

The meaning of leadership under study in this chapter is consistent with the definition provided by John Kotter[4]: "Leadership defines what the future should look like, aligns people with that vision, and inspires them to make it happen despite the obstacles." It is distinctly different from "management," which is more concerned with processes that keep a complicated system of people and technology running smoothly. Activities such as planning, budgeting, organizing, staffing, controlling, and problem-solving are central to the task of management. Leaders are involved in carrying out their organization's vision, which increasingly depends on their customers. An organization's vision cannot be easily separated from its "brand," or set of brands, and the ensuing conversations about the brand with current and potential customers.

Every leader will be different in his or her approach to driving an organization. Henry Ford, who founded the Ford Motor Company, offers a provocative example of a leader. He created the first widely known auto brand (Ford) available to customers, revolutionized manufacturing with the assembly line, and developed fair worker compensation built around a five-day work week. Despite these accomplishments, Ford's reported controversial personality involving labor union problems, pacifism during World War 1, and anti-Semitism tarnished the Ford brand in a way that enabled competitors to gain a strong foothold in the market.[5] Research shows that customers connect leaders intimately with their brands. As concluded in one study[6]:

Respondents construed [CEOs] presence in ads as a credible indication of the extent to which [they are] committed to their products, not to mention the degree to which they are willing to take responsibility for the brand. In terms of gaining the hearts and minds of their targeted customers, CEOs seem to have a special advantage ... people feel a unique connection to them.

The brand does not have to carry the CEO's name, but the brand messages should provide an opportunity to link the CEO with the brand to humanize it and provide a platform for conversation. In this chapter, the tragic fate of three brands in the retail sector is considered: RadioShack, Borders, and Circuit City. Each provides an understanding of the important role of leaders and patterns of leadership in dynamically changing markets. While the impact of technology myopia, ruptured loyalties, bruising viral spirals, and catastrophes can have a devastating impact on many firms and their brands, it becomes clear from the following three cases that a crisis can come from the inside as well as the outside.

RadioShack Corporation: Leadership Gone Radio Silent

Ironically, because brands can outlive people, changes in leadership can create opportunities or problems for a brand. As often occurs, leadership changes are correlated with changes in the market environment, especially as those changes influence customers and their behavior. Take the case of RadioShack, founded in 1921 by brothers Theodore and Milton Deutschmann to provide amateur radio equipment to home hobbyists. In 1947, it opened its first audio equipment showroom and during the 1950s, expanded into music equipment and opened nine stores. However, due to operational difficulties in the early 1960s, it approached bankruptcy and in 1963 was purchased by the Tandy Corporation to expand further into the hobbyist market.

Under the leadership of Charles Tandy, the management of RadioShack was substantially improved. Tandy continued building the RadioShack brand name and maintained its brand relationship with hobbyist customers, spending as much as nine percent of its sales on advertising and expanding the number of retail stores. It focused on the needs of its hobbyist customers by offering the latest technologies. For example, it was the most popular place to acquire citizen band (CB) radios, a craze in the 1970s, and radar speed detectors. In 1977, it launched the TRS80, one of the first hobbyist personal computers that even outsold Apple II, Apple's initial computer. In 1978, Charles Tandy passed away, but the firm's operations continued under its management team.[7]

A new CEO was announced in 1981 and served until the end of 1998. During this time, Tandy RadioShack was under the leadership of the same CEO who was able to expand retail stores to take advantage of several technology trends, including personal computers, landline phones, and mobile phones. The period was characterized by entering and exiting a variety of business situations. Tracking RadioShack's performance based on its split-adjusted stock price during the tenure of this CEO (noted as CEO1 in Figure 6.1) reveals a rather steady valuation of the business when expectations were growing for improved performance.

As the chart in Figure 6.1 shows, after 1999, a serious decline in the value of RadioShack became obvious. Over the next 15 years, until its bankruptcy in 2015, RadioShack experienced six different CEOs, each with different views and approaches to improve business. A few of the problems faced over this time included the following:

- Few of the CEOs had any frontline customer-facing experience in electronics. Most came from backgrounds that did not include the

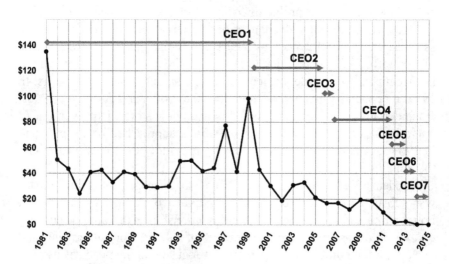

Figure 6.1.   RadioShack Year Ending Stock Price with CEO Changes Noted

Source: Stock price data from: http://www.1stock1.com/1stock1_236.htm (Accessed December 13, 2022); CEO data from various sources.

dynamic characteristics of RadioShack's customers and electronic products and services.

- A CEO submitted his resignation to the board of directors over allegations that he had falsified his education on his curriculum vitae; the allegations were subsequently confirmed.[8]
- Store managers were frustrated by RadioShack's "Fix 1500" initiative. The program graded and ranked them on eight criteria based on interviews with district managers. Consequently, in 2004 alone, some 1,700 managers were reassigned or terminated. The program resulted in several civil action suits from disgruntled employees.[9]
- Customer in-store experiences were reportedly unpleasant, often alienating truly loyal RadioShack customers. In 2011, one rating company ranked RadioShack last in terms of customer experience among 27 major US retailers.[10]
- Employees became unhappy when they were required to shift their activities from providing superior electronics advice to meet the needs of their loyal hobbyist customers to pursuing sales of computers, phones, and service contracts with higher profit margins.[11]

Some of the main reasons for RadioShack's demise were influenced by increased competition from major computer and mobile phone firms. The company tried a variety of new retail operations, none of which gained traction. Every new leader brought a different tactic to succeed, none of which connected with their core market of customers: the hobbyist. As one article succinctly noted: "RadioShack suffered from poor, often overpaid, leadership, which could not focus on a single plan and then was left grasping for a rescue strategy."[12] The article went on to offer what might have been possible if the leadership of RadioShack had been more strategic in terms of placing a greater focus on the customer in their business[13]:

> RadioShack tried many paths. But going in all directions without a full commitment is not enough, particularly when the core brand is not sustained. RadioShack has branded itself well but it led itself too far from its strengths.

Sadly, in 2015, RadioShack and its troubled pattern of leadership went radio silent into bankruptcy. Its dissolution left many people unhappy and sent its customers in search of other retail brands in hopes of a more beneficial relationship and connectivity to meet their needs. The opportunity to stay focused on the so-called "hobbyist" customer may not have been so much about specific types of people but about the need for the hobbyist experience that exists in many customers. The change from the original strategy of Charles Tandy with a clear focus on the hobbyist customer to the subsequent efforts by a parade of seven different leaders illustrates the dire consequences of leadership lost.

Borders Group Inc.: Closed Book on Leadership

In 1971, Louis and Tom Borders founded Borders as a single store selling used books in Ann Arbor, Michigan, a college town that was home to the University of Michigan.[14] To manage the purchasing of books, they also developed a book inventory system (BIS) that enabled them to efficiently and effectively order and stock books. The importance of this for meeting customer needs cannot be underestimated. If a customer wants a specific book that is not available or locatable in the store, a sale may be lost and more importantly, the customer may not return to the store for other books. Furthermore, the system enabled each store to provide more customized offerings to its shoppers. The BIS was eventually computerized and became its own separate business.

By 1988, Borders had five stores in the Midwest, 14 bookstore clients through BIS, and a net income of $1.9 million. Borders also built its first "superstore" concept in the mid-1980s, which took the idea of a small bookstore into a superstore concept that could become a chain of retail stores. In 1992, seeing the success of Borders in book retailing, Kmart purchased the chain of stores to add to its recently acquired Waldenbooks retail chain. In 1994, Borders and Waldenbooks merged to form Borders Group Inc. and went public in May 1995 under the leadership of Robert DiRomualdo, who was hired by the Borders brothers in 1988 to help manage and grow the business.

At the core of Borders' success were its customers and how they were treated. By tracking the books and music that its customers wanted, it could replenish quickly with its inventory system and make sure customers' needs were met. In the pre-digital marketplace of purchasing books, it was of substantial value for a customer to peruse large numbers of books, handle them, and decide whether to buy on the spot.

Managers and employees of each store were required to be college graduates who were tested and trained on various literary topics to better serve customers. Customer service was a priority and included help in finding books, conducting book and poetry readings, and other community-based literary activities for children and adults. Customer service was also extended in many stores with comfortable seating areas and espresso bars.

The company grew rapidly from 1995 to 1998 with the development of 256 superstores. During this period, they expanded large portions of each store into the merchandising of music and video. They also acquired various video retail chains and began to divest several unprofitable Walden bookstores among some of the 900 located in traditional shopping malls. Beginning in 1997, it acquired a chain of small bookstores in London and subsequently expanded its international presence. All of these acquisitive activities plus the parallel actions of Barnes & Noble, a major competitor with a similar offering, drove many of the smaller independent bookstores out of business. Yet, during this time, Amazon, which began marketing books in 1994, slowly began to catch the eye and trust of the reading public and its sales grew.

In mid-1998 to compete with Amazon, Borders.com was launched as part of its "Borders Online" operation. It was designed to provide customers with opportunities to search for titles and determine their availability in stores or through Borders.com for purchase. In its first year, it generated $4.6 million in online revenue relative to Amazon's $610 million and Barnes & Noble's $63 million in online revenue.[15] Although well intentioned, the accuracy of data on books in the stores was ultimately problematic, thereby frustrating customers. About this time, Amazon launched the sale of music and videos, along with its growing book business, putting additional pressure on Borders' brick-and-mortar stores.

Unfortunately, Borders.com did not perform well. While it was launched during the 2000 dot.com bust, it had continuing operational issues and faced aggressive competition. After three years of sub-optimal website revenues, in 2001, Borders' leadership struck a deal with Amazon to partner in the e-commerce space.[16] This agreement placed Amazon in control of the operations of the website with Borders receiving a percentage of the sales. Borders' management team believed the partnership with Amazon allowed Borders to continue its focus on brick-and-mortar stores yet also having a Borders branded online presence through Amazon.[17] Unfortunately, the terms of the agreement favored Amazon. Perhaps more importantly, the reliance on Amazon distracted Borders leadership from pursuing an aggressive digital strategy during the time when it was necessary to meet customer needs and be competitive. Ultimately, this allowed Barnes & Noble to become the second largest online provider of books.

For Borders leadership, abandoning a stronger capability in online book marketing to Amazon.com and Barnes & Noble was a fatal flaw in its approach to its business and customers. Its continued pursuit of acquiring traditional bookstores in the US and internationally from 2001 to 2006 enhanced the year-to-year financials but ignored the needs and preferences of customers to purchase books online conveniently and informatively — a process that Amazon had mastered. Subsequently, a lack of clear leadership and vision led to a litany of problems that drained the life out of Borders:

- Lost sales to online purchases (especially from Amazon.com) plus the costs of labor, inventory, and stockouts for their superstores put tremendous financial pressure on their operations.
- Leaders did not anticipate the rapid growth of Starbucks, which provided customers with an alternative place to a bookstore to have an espresso, relax, and read.
- Other mass merchandise retailers (e.g., Walmart and Target) sold the most popular books, which drained revenue from Borders.
- The growth of Apple's iPod and iTunes drove a decline in traditional retail music sales (CDs), which further eroded Border's revenue.

The year 2006 was the last profitable one for Borders. In 2008, Borders Group management began exploring the option of merging with competitor Barnes & Noble. At the start of 2010, the company announced that it would begin significant job cuts and close down several stores. Eventually, in 2012, the company filed for Chapter 11. As indicated by Borders historical stock performance (see Figure 6.2), it can be surmised that the explosive growth of the Internet and financial crisis of 2008 created environments in which Borders Group and its leadership could not thrive.

In its 15 years of existence as a public company from 1995 to 2011, Borders experienced seven CEO changes (in one case, the same CEO came back for a short period to replace one departure). The CEO changes along with the stock price are plotted in the chart in Figure 6.2. The pattern is somewhat similar to Radio Shack: a rapid series of leadership changes just before the firm's final demise. Although each brand lived in

Figure 6.2.   Borders Group Year Ending Stock Price with CEO Changes Noted

Source: Stock price data from: https://ih.advfn.com/stock-market/NYSE/borders-BGP/stock-price, (Accessed July 30, 2021); CEO data from various sources.

different markets, their customer behaviors were strongly influenced by similar market dynamics, e.g., rapid technology changes, new and powerful online competitors, and difficult economic conditions.

Leaders were at a loss to cope with these challenges. The best chance they had was to capitalize on the strength of its brand relationships with its customer base to build a strong online presence in the early days of Amazon. Barnes & Noble just managed to survive because of its online presence and its Nook e-book reader. In 2019, it was purchased by a firm from the United Kingdom with the intent of continuing the survival of the Barnes & Noble brand to its customer base. The new CEO of Barnes & Noble, James Daunt, planned to revive the bookstore brand by going from a mass merchandiser of the same book inventory to a more local approach, which allows local store managers to remain closer to the customer — an approach that enables better brand connectivity with customers.[18]

Circuit City Corporation: "Good to Great to Gone"

In his book *Good to Great to Gone*, Alan Wurtzel, the son of Sam Wurtzel the founder of Circuit City, described his perspectives on its 60-year rise and fall.[19] What is most important about the book is the emphasis placed on the importance of leadership and how it drives strategy, the ultimate arbiter of business performance. Wurtzel offers the concept of "habits of mind," which clearly plants the origin of strategy into the mind of a firm's leader and its leadership. The title of his book plays on the work of Jim Collins' book: *Good to Great*,[20] in which Circuit City was identified as one of the "great" companies. Regrettably, it met with failure.

Circuit City began as "Wards Company," a television retail store founded in 1949 by Sam Wurtzel. As an entrepreneur, Wurtzel capitalized on the emerging television industry. He initially offered Olympic brand television sets through advertising in the classified ad section of local newspapers. By 1959, Wards' business expanded beyond television into home appliances and operated four stores with annual sales of $1 million. During the 1960s, the company grew through the acquisition of a variety of television and home appliance stores and by 1968, moved from the over-the-counter exchange to the American Stock Exchange.

Beginning in 1970, Alan Wurtzel followed his father, the founding CEO, to become the new CEO of Circuit City. He recognized the importance of better managing the diverse portfolio of stores and the brand names he inherited. He also had to manage the economic decline of the early 1970s. To do so, he developed a strategic plan that recognized the growing trend of the "warehouse showroom" retail concept, of which Levitz Furniture was a prime example at the time. This type of "superstore" involved showing customers the products on the showroom floor, allowing them to ask salespeople for help or explanations, and then allowing them to easily make their purchase and take it home immediately or have it delivered. In addition, recognition of the demographics and trends in music from the 1960s into the 1970s drove Wurtzel and his team to include a variety of high-fidelity sound equipment along with video, appliances, and other electronic products in their new stores.

The superstore concept enabled Wurtzel and his team to consolidate all their various stores and names into a coherent brand and location strategy. To support the drive to build these superstores, the firm consulted with an agency to rename the brand from Wards to Circuit City in 1977. This avoided confusion and litigation with Montgomery Ward's department stores. The new stores enabled Circuit City to capitalize on the rapid growth of appliances and eventually personal computers, monitors, and their accessories going into the 1980s.

The objective of the superstores was to provide customers with an unparalleled shopping and purchasing experience both in terms of store design and salesperson help. The customer focus was defined by their 5-S's of Savings, Selection, Service, Satisfaction, and Speed. In 1984, with growing financial success and an emerging strong brand, Circuit City moved from the American Stock Exchange to the New York Stock Exchange. The brand relationship between Circuit City and its customers was established. In 1986, with this success Wurtzel stepped down as CEO.

The new CEO believed there were limitations to Circuit City's growth going into the mid-1980s and 1990s brought on by the saturation of major markets with their superstores. Consequently, in 1993, the new CEO decided to diversify the company's portfolio by creating a used-car retailer called CarMax. The early days of CarMax were difficult (it did not turn its first annual profit until the year 2000),[21] although its development eventually paid off, but not for Circuit City.

Then, in 1995, the CEO began to explore a digital video concept ultimately called DIVX as an alternative to VHS home video players. It launched in 1998, but without substantial support from the movie studios to cooperate, the venture failed in 1999 at a loss of $220 million after taxes.[22] The loss was substantial but not crippling to the firm. Of greater concern was the loss of focus on the core Circuit City business by its leadership.

While Circuit City leadership was pursuing its other ventures, during the 1980s and into the early 1990s, a strong competitor was emerging: BestBuy. Although the firm was not as profitable as Circuit City during this time, and perhaps not appearing to be a threat, it followed a process of continuous improvement. The leadership of BestBuy intensively studied the market and customer shopping behaviors, especially the limitations of Circuit City stores. This evolved into a BestBuy in-store experience that customers preferred over Circuit City.

This did not happen overnight for BestBuy, but it occurred through a series of at least four different "concept stores." Each store was a successive improvement on how to bring about changes that helped customers better meet their needs. For example, they learned that customers were becoming confused by the dizzying array of technologies arriving in the stores. So, instead of using traditional salespeople (which Circuit City depended upon), BestBuy provided technical support people in the stores to help customers better understand the new technologies. Continuing to meet the need for technical support, BestBuy acquired a company called the Geek Squad, which provided customers with in-home installation services of the more technical products, a service that turned out to be highly profitable for BestBuy.

BestBuy was not the death knell for Circuit City but leadership taking its eyes off customers and the brand led Alan Wurtzel to summarize the beginning of the end[23]:

> While sales and profits grew and the stock reached an all-time high in 2000, under Circuit City's hood was an aging store base, a failing marketing strategy, an expensive workforce, and an increasingly out-of-date management information system.

Dropping to second place behind BestBuy in terms of overall sales, sales-per-store, sales per square foot, and profit by 2000 cost Circuit City its premier position in deal-making with vendors. It eventually dropped to third place after BestBuy and Walmart in terms of sales of electronic products. Leadership pursuing other ventures and taking eyes off the core business with its customers and brand allowed a strong competitor to emerge. With all of these challenges percolating for Circuit City, even with the stock price at an all-time high at the beginning of 2000 (see Figure 6.3), the CEO appointed in 2000 faced the challenge of whether or not it could make a comeback.

The key actions taken by the new CEO in 2000 and two others who followed brought the eventual demise of Circuit City. A summary of some critical factors contributing to the downfall of Circuit City revolves around the impact it had on the brand and its customers in terms of a failing connectivity with them.[24]

- **Focusing on a Narrower Segment of the Market:** According to "Circuit City Stores Inc., Fully Integrated Marketing 3-year Plan, FY 2001–2003" cited by Wurtzel, the core customer was defined as "those individuals who value leading edge technologies and the sales assisted service we provide."[25] Clearly, the push was on its higher technology-oriented customers, ignoring a larger segment of more basic customers and their needs for essential appliances and electronic products.
- **Exiting the Appliance Market:** With the technology-focused customer in mind, and the lower profitability of selling appliances, in

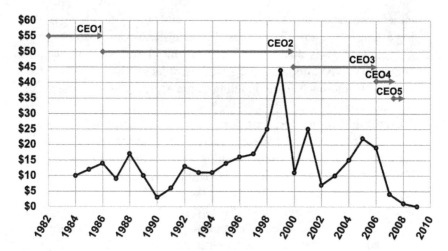

Figure 6.3.   Circuit City Year Ending Stock Price with CEO Changes Noted

Source: Stock price data from TheStockMarketWatch.com. https://thestockmarketwatch.com/stock/ stock-data.aspx?symbol=CCTYQ&action=showHistory&page=1&perPage=25&startMonth=0&start Day=1&startYear=2011&endMonth=11&endDay=31&endYear=2011&endDateLite=07%2F26 %2F2020 (Accessed July 30, 2021). CEO data from Wurtzel, Alan L., Good to Great to Gone, New York: Diversion Books, 2012.

2001, Circuit City stopped selling appliances in its stores. While the financial rationale for such a decision could be supported, customers still needed appliances and when they could not find them at Circuit City, they shopped elsewhere — where appliances were available, as well as electronics and other related technology products — thereby breaking the connection with the brand.

- **Stumbling on Store Remodeling:** To be more competitive with BestBuy's store designs and merchandising layout, the new Circuit City leader pushed for new store concepts and designs. The abandonment of selling appliances provided the in-store space to reconceptualize the layout. A model was developed (code-named "Horizon") in Jacksonville, Florida. Despite poor early sales results, the process to remodel continued. Another concept store ("Tide") was developed in St. Petersburg, Florida, with favorable results. However, taking any concept store and using it as a model to change all stores in a chain. without recognizing the complexities involved can be risky. Changing the structure of a store meant either closing it entirely or partially — in either case generating sales and possible customer loss. Doing so during a time when a firm's business financials and competitive position are unfavorable is difficult. After these initial attempts to develop a comprehensive remodeling program, the process was abandoned for a piecemeal approach to remodeling some stores, closing others, and leaving others alone.

- **Unsettling Employees:** For many, the well-trained sales force of Circuit City was a major advantage over BestBuy. Sales force training was essential to the quality and productivity of its sales force. However, beginning in 2001, the team of 25 human trainers was replaced by online training as a cost-saving effort — gone were the important steps of real-time practice and peer feedback. Then, in 2002, the variable commission structure (by product line) was replaced by a fixed commission structure, irritating many people in the sales force. To reduce expenses further, in 2003, it completely eliminated commission selling and fired 3,900 of its highest paid salespeople. They were replaced by 2,100 new hourly workers. While it is debatable whether this represented a long overdue decision to be competitive with BestBuy, who used hourly workers, or whether it was the loss of a differentiating competitive advantage, the timing and the way in which the process was managed certainly created turmoil among employees about job security and the future of the firm.

- **Buying and Selling Businesses:** Going into the 21st century under financial pressure was not a good place for a new CEO to be. To raise capital for potential store remodeling and expansion in 2002, the firm spun off CarMax raising $140 million. In 2004, Circuit City acquired InterTAN, a Canadian firm that operated almost 1,000 RadioShack stores. Ironically, RadioShack sued Circuit City over its name, resulting in Circuit City renaming the Canadian store chain to "The Source by Circuit City." Unfortunately, the chain did not provide the planned financial returns. Near the end of 2003, Circuit City sold its Visa and MasterCard businesses to banks, generating cash for operations.

Taken together, all these activities were implemented in some form or another to turn around the business. It did so for a brief time in 2005 and 2006 when sales and profitability increased. However, this was due more to an increase in new flat panel television sales than a more efficient and effective overall business performance. With new short-term CEOs in 2006 and 2007, very little could be done to halt the market leadership of

BestBuy and other competitors. The succession of leaders and actions from 2000 forward could not overturn the loss of customers to a competitive brand that did a much better job of generating brand connectivity with its customers. On November 10, 2008, Circuit City filed for bankruptcy.

Leadership Lost in Transition

The three case studies presented in this chapter suggest the possibility that leaders, especially their transitions, can move their organizations into brand tragedies despite their best intentions. RadioShack, Borders, and Circuit City — once great brands that built strong relationships with their customers — are gone! The loss of products and services to meet customer needs is one aspect of the loss, but perhaps more immediate in many cases are the losses for employees, shareholders, and suppliers.

Not surprisingly, one of the important threads that runs through all the cases in this chapter and the book is *leadership*. Providing an organization with a clear vision of the future linked to a strategy that connects its brand with its customers is a critical function of leadership. The three cases presented in this chapter provide the basis for a signpost of three factors to remember why it's important to stay focused on a brand's leaders as a potential source of a brand tragedy. These factors include staying truly close to the customer, building strategic agility into the organization, and carefully orchestrating leadership transitions.

Leaders Must Stay Close to the Customer

Among the key dimensions of any worthwhile business is the importance of staying close to the customer. Customers are the lifeline to a firm's business success. Understanding customers and their needs is central to business performance. Unfortunately, customers are more easily neglected relative to other organizational challenges. Perhaps, the main reason for this is that customers are often geographically located far away from the organizations and leaders that serve them. The relative immediacy of the demands from nearby managers, employees, shareholders, and others can easily distract leaders from spending time with their customers.

In each of the three cases, RadioShack, Border's, and Circuit City, the founders were successful because they were physically close to their customers in their initial retail stores. They could observe, interact, communicate, and otherwise directly engage people in their stores to better learn their needs. However, as the number of stores increased, the founders and their subsequent leaders could easily become removed from the face-to-face connectivity with customers. Furthermore, as in the case of RadioShack, few of the next generation of leaders had any frontline customer-facing experience in electronics relative to the early founders, a contributing factor to its downfall.

This is not just true for retailers but for any kind of organization that involves meeting a customer's need. Staying close to the customer is essential, but how to do so when physical distance becomes difficult? In some ways, if the COVID-19 pandemic brought any benefit, it was the increased ability to connect virtually with almost anyone anywhere who possessed Internet access. There is absolutely no reason for organizational leaders, especially CEOs, to be remote from their customers.

Leaders must learn how to directly connect and interact with customers in-person and virtually as often as possible. A minimum once-a-week 30-minute conversation with customers would produce some 50 customer conversations in a year. Imagine the value it can bring if several C-Suite leaders conducted similar brand conversations with customers and then used technology to compare notes and identify critical issues and opportunities for their brands!

Leaders Must Build Strategic Agility into their Organizations

On one hand, "strategic agility" may seem like a buzzword that can be easily dismissed; but on the other hand, if practiced well, it may be the only way to deal with fast-moving businesses, markets, and customers. Three critical factors determine strategic agility for an organization: how well its leaders *develop and evolve a strategy* built on a successful business model, how well they *empower their people to act with agility*, and how well they provide access to superb *information technology* (IT) to sense and respond to its environment, especially competition.

In each of the three cases in this chapter, the founders and immediate successive leaders built a successful business model. Continuing the success required an evolving strategy of their business models in response to external factors. Strategy is the long-term (usually three to five years) direction of an organization that leads to a competitive advantage and creates sustainable value for its stakeholders. A strategy facilitates and points to the implementation of day-to-day actions. Furthermore, it's not just about competitive marketing strategy, or customer strategy, but a clear, focused, and integrated business strategy that drives marketing, operations, manufacturing, finance, human resources, and other key business functions.

In all three case studies, the various leaders diverged from their core business strategies in response to external threats rather than carefully reviewing the current strategy and revising certain actions in an agile manner. This is especially important for a brand and its customer base. RadioShack abandoned its hobbyist customer focus; Circuit City targeted a new technology-savvy customer, abandoning its traditional "bread-and-butter" customers; and Borders abandoned customers who were looking for a different way to obtain their books and reading experiences.

Strategy must be accompanied by organizational agility to succeed. Organizational agility is based on the idea of establishing a capability to rapidly sense and respond to a threat or capitalize on an opportunity presented by aggressive competitors and other market changes.[26] Agility is not just about rapidly changing something but carefully sensing what needs to be changed in the context of current strategy and then revising accordingly. It was imperative for Borders to respond rapidly and forcefully to the growing threat of Amazon.com. It was not something that would be easy; nevertheless, it was something Barnes & Noble managed to achieve, but Borders did not.

Agility occurs "when people are engaged, ready to take on new challenges, open and generating new ideas, learning and feeling vital, all of which describe a state of thriving."[27] People organized in agile teams are empowered to uncover threats and opportunities and make the necessary changes to respond. With a strong business foundation in place and empowered teams, the responses can be innovative, surprising, adaptable, and/or resilient.

The third key factor to support strategic agility is that data must be available to sense an opportunity or threat, thereby enabling a team to evaluate the situation and shape the response. Acquisition of the right kind and amount of data at the right time involves an IT support system that meets the requirements of the agile teams. For example, a "customer team" will require timely data and insights that enable tracking numerous metrics on customer behaviors, especially as it relates to the brand. A "competitive team" will require timely data on traditional and newly emerging competitors and the customers they are targeting. Data collection capabilities, cloud data storage, predictive models, machine learning, artificial intelligence, interactive communication, statistical software, and numerous other IT tools and methods are required to provide the kind of agility teams need to sense market changes and take proper actions.

To summarize, recall Alan Wurtzel's "habits of mind" in his book describing Circuit City's ultimate demise; it focused on the importance of leadership and strategy.[28] It was based on three key ideas. The first was "confront the brutal facts," which in the Circuit City case meant that leadership did not completely have the right information to understand its dire financial situation from the early 2000s to their bankruptcy in 2008. His second was to "mind the culture," which meant creating the equivalent of an agile organization in which employees were respected and allowed to make mistakes without fear of punishment, something that did not happen in the 2000 and beyond version of Circuit City. His third was "pass the torch with care," which meant properly managing the transition of CEOs and other leaders, something missing in each of the case studies and considered as a third key factor defining the leadership signpost.

Leaders Must Carefully Orchestrate their Transitions

The patterns of stock prices and CEO leadership changes in Figures 6.1–6.3 expose the risks of leadership transition: Consider the following patterns of CEO tenure from the year 2000 to bankruptcy:

- **RadioShack:** six changes from 2000 to 2016 (2.7 years average tenure);
- **Borders Group:** four changes from 2000 to 2011 (2.8 years average tenure);
- **Circuit City:** three changes from 2000 to 2008 (2.7 years average tenure).

In a study of 356 firms between 2000 and 2010, researchers found an "average" tenure length of 7.6 years and an "optimal" tenure length of 4.8 years.[29] Optimal length was defined by factors such as the strength of the firm–employee relationships, customer relationships, and the magnitude and volatility of stock returns. Clearly, the three case studies considered in this chapter reveal below average tenure lengths, whether measured absolutely or optimally.

These findings do not suggest that transition metrics alone are the cause of success or failure but rather that CEO leadership transition can be a critical factor in a firm's performance. The three firms considered in this chapter are all retail chains, and their demise was seemingly correlated with the post 2000 rise in technology. This could explain their transition difficulties, however other firms in their industries have survived during this time: BestBuy and Barnes & Noble, for example. It could also be that the number of CEO transitions accelerates only when firms are in strategic and financial difficulty — which of course implies that strategies and other actions had broken down.

Firms that expect to have an ongoing and productive customer relationship through their brands must have a clear and planned leadership transition plan. This may involve the board of directors and other key organizational stakeholders. The responsibility for new leadership success is not just with the new leader but with the plan that brings about the transition. The plan should include clarity on several factors, including the business strategy, the culture, the teams, recruiting capabilities, and other stakeholders that need to be managed.[30] Unfortunately, studies show that some 27–46 percent of leadership transitions are failures or disappointments two years after the change.[31]

Propositions to Consider in Developing a Signpost for Leadership Lost

The three factors considered above to foster the development of a signpost for leadership lost are briefly summarized here as propositions:

- **Leaders Must Stay Close to Customers:** The greater the distance between leaders and customers, the greater the vulnerability to a brand tragedy.
- **Leaders Must Build Strategic Agility in their Organizations:** The less capable leaders are to build agile organizations, the greater the vulnerability to a brand tragedy.
- **Leaders Must Carefully Orchestrate Their Transitions:** The weaker the orchestration of leadership transitions (especially at the C-Suite level), the greater the vulnerability to a brand tragedy.

While there may be several reasons for failures in leadership, it is an outcome that might be expected. Organizations come to life to bring order, structure, and stability to the behaviors of people and the necessary activities that must be accomplished for success. Ironically, the need to be strategic, agile, and able to change by its leaders may be hampered by the very natural process to maintain stability. In effect, the organization becomes imprisoned by its own structure. As will be seen in Chapter 7, this roadblock to change is considered a key reason why leadership may be difficult and another reason why brand tragedies occur.

Endnotes

1. Kapner, Suzanne, "Amazon Didn't Cripple Bed Bath & Beyond. Its Own Leaders Did," *The Wall Street Journal*, June 13, 2019. https://www.wsj.com/articles/amazon-didnt-cripple-bed-bath-beyond-its-own-leaders-did-11559467800 (Accessed May 24, 2022).
2. Ryan, Tracy, "Tech Titans Face Antitrust Questions," *The Wall Street Journal*, July 30, 2020, P. 1+.
3. Friederichsen, Paul, "How CEO's Shape Brand Perceptions," *Branding Strategy Insider*, September 27, 2016. www.brandingstrategyinsider.com/2016/09/how-ceos-shape-brand-perceptions.html#.WsKl_dPwbdR (Accessed May 24, 2022).
4. Kotter, J. P., *Leading Change*. Boston: Harvard Business School Press, 1996.
5. Friederichsen, *Op. cit.*
6. Fleck, Nathalie, Geraldine Michel and Valerie Zeitounet, "Brand Personification Through the Use of Spokespeople: An Exploratory Study of Ordinary Employees, CEOs, and Celebrities Featured in Advertising," *Psychology & Marketing*, 31(1), January 2014, 84–92, 87.
7. "Tandy Corporation," International Directory of Company Histories, *Encyclopedia.com*. https://www.encyclopedia.com/books/politics-and-business-magazines/tandy-corporation (Accessed May 24, 2022).
8. "RadioShack CEO's Resume Raises Questions," *NBCNews.com*, NBCUniversal News Group, 15 February 2006, www.nbcnews.com/id/11354888/.
9. World Heritage Encyclopedia, "Tandy Radio Shack." Wikipedia contributors, "RadioShack," *Wikipedia, The Free Encyclopedia*, https://

en.wikipedia.org/w/index.php?title=RadioShack&oldid=1148128164 (Accessed April 4, 2023).

10. Temkin Ratings, "Amazon.com Leads, RadioShack Lags Retail Customer Experience," June 22, 2011. https://experiencematters.blog/category/temkin-ratings/2011-temkin-ratings/ (Accessed May 24, 2022).

11. Bloomberg News. "Inside RadioShack's Slow-Motion Collapse: Why the Fall of the 94-Year-Old Electronics Chain Didn't Have to Be This Way," *Financial Post*, February 16, 2015.

12. Solomon, Steven D., "For RadioShack, a Long History of Misses and Missteps," *New York Times*, September 16, 2014, p. B5.

13. *Ibid.*, p. B5.

14. The historical aspects of this section up to the year 2001 are based on: "Borders Group, Inc. — Company Profile, Information, Business Description, History, Background Information on Borders Group, Inc.," *Reference for Business, Company History Index*. https://www.referenceforbusiness.com/history2/83/Borders-Group-Inc.html (Accessed May 24, 2022).

15. Ton, Zeynep and Ananth Raman, *Borders Group, Inc.* HBS Number 9-601-037, Boston: Harvard Business School Publishing, 2000.

16. "Timeline: A Short History of Borders Group Bookstores." *Reuters*, February 16, 2011. www.reuters.com/article/us-borders-timeline/timeline-a-short-history-of-borders-group-bookstores-idUSTRE-71F3AT20110216 (Accessed May 24, 2022).

17. Levinson, Meredith. "Borders Tries to Open New Chapter with Website Relaunch Separate from Amazon.Com." *CIO*, October 2, 2007. https://www.cio.com/article/2437960/borders-tries-to-open-new-chapter-with-website-relaunch-separate-from-amazon-com.html (Accessed August 1, 2020).

18. Trachtenberg, Jeffrey A., "Barnes & Noble's New Boss Tries to Save the Chain — And Traditional Bookselling," *Wall Street Journal*, December 5, 2020. https://www.wsj.com/articles/barnes-nobles-new-boss-tries-to-save-the-chainand-traditional-bookselling-11607144485?mod=searchresults_pos1&page=1 (Accessed March 1, 2023).

19. The brief background of Circuit City in this section is based on: Wurtzel, Alan L., *Good to Great to Gone*. New York: Diversion Books, 2012.

20. Collins, Jim, *Good to Great*. New York: Harper Collins, 2001.

21. Wurtzel, *Op. cit.*, p. 288.

22. Fost, Dan, "Divx's Death Pleases Opponents," *San Francisco Chronicle*, June 18, 1999, p. B-2.
23. Wurtzel, *Op. cit.*, p. 245.
24. This section is based on Wurtzel, *Op. cit.*, and Wells, John R. and Galen Danskin, *The Fall of Circuit City Stores Inc.* HBS 9-713-402, Boston: Harvard Business Publishing, 2012.
25. Wurtzel, *Op. cit.*, p. 257.
26. Goldman, S. L., R. N. Nagel, and K. Preiss, *Agile Competitors and Virtual Organizations: Strategies for Enriching the Customer*. New York: Van Nostrand Reinhold, 1994.
27. Keister, Angela C. C., "Thriving Teams and Change Agility: Leveraging a Collective State to Create Organization Agility," *Research in Organizational Change and Development*, Vol. 22. Bingley, UK: Emerald Group Publishing Limited, July 23, 2014, pp. 299–333.
28. Wurtzel, *Op. cit.*, p. 333.
29. Xueming, Luo, Vamsi K. Kanuri, and Michelle Andrews, "Long CEO Tenure Can Hurt Performance," *Harvard Business Review*, 91(3), 2013, 26–27.
30. Keller, Scott and Mary Meaney, "Successfully Transitioning to New Leadership Roles," *McKinsey & Company*, May 23, 2018. https://www.mckinsey.com/business-functions/organization/our-insights/successfully-transitioning-to-new-leadership-roles (Accessed May 24, 2022).
31. *Ibid.*

Chapter 7

Psychic Prisons

In his book *Images of Organizations*, Gareth Morgan highlights the importance of understanding the behavior of organizations through *metaphors*.[1] Although he cautions that misusing a metaphor to explain organizational behavior can provide only a partial and possibly distorted view, he argues that metaphors can provide deeper insights into how organizations work. He considers organizations metaphorically as cultures, organisms, brains, and political systems, among others. The point is that by understanding various metaphors, one can gain a more profound understanding of why organizations behave the way they do (e.g., fall into the trap of technology myopia) and how to better manage them.

One of Morgan's often overlooked metaphors is the organization as a *psychic prison*. The concept of the psychic prison derives from the idea that "favored ways of thinking and acting become traps that confine individuals within socially constructed worlds and prevent the emergence of other worlds."[2] One would expect that as something new from the outside begins to disrupt current patterns, it increases the tendency to incorporate it into the current mode of thinking but not in the case of a psychic prison. A clear example of a kind of psychic prison from Chapter 2 was BlackBerry's response to the Apple iPhone with the touchscreen. Rather than adopt Apple's approach to touchscreens BlackBerry chose to retain as much of the mechanical QWERTY keyboard "touch and feel" as possible in its Storm phone, which unfortunately resulted in technical difficulties and customer problems.

In the context of brand tragedies, an organization that finds it difficult to change in response to threats to its brand relationships with customers may lead to a brand's tragic demise. For example, how could VisiCalc have allowed an employee to develop a better spreadsheet and then leave to start a new company (Lotus 1-2-3)? Psychic prisons may provide a partial answer to these questions. The psychic prison metaphor may be at the heart of what Thomas described as the "new product development paradox" within organizations:

> The new product development paradox recognizes that strong motivating forces of change propel new product development and that these motivating forces also often stimulate countervailing forces of resistance to change that may stifle the product's evolution.[3]

He described the example of Motorola's 1990–1991 delay in developing a RISC computer chip to meet the needs of customers. As reported in the *Wall Street Journal*, Motorola's "obsession with excellence" and "infighting" between champions of the very successful existing 68,000 series chip versus a new RISC chip technology may have delayed the launch of its new products by a year after competitors launched their products.[4] In this case, one part of the organization struggled to maintain the success of its 68,000 chip and put itself in a prison cell of resisting change. Another part of the firm was clearly aware of the new RISC technologies available and pursued product development on it. When the RISC group put pressure on the 68000 group to change, this established yet another prison cell leading to infighting that slowed their response to competitors.

As Morgan noted in his book, no single metaphor should explain an organization's behavior, but the psychic prisons that managers may create around their successes and reasons for not changing are compelling ones. In Morgan's description of psychic prisons, it is important to note that there is more than one type, even within a single organization. These will be referred to as psychic prison "cells." For example, there can be a technology prison cell, a marketing prison cell, an operations prison cell, and possibly others. This is similar to a siloed organizational structure in some ways, but can also happen within silos. In such organizations, brand relationships with customers from only the marketing unit may be of little help without cooperation from other parts of the organization. In this chapter, the case studies of Nokia and Kodak reveal the characteristics of psychic prisons and the tragic impact on their brands.

Nokia: Imprisoned in Fear

After an historic start as a paper mill in 1865, Nokia ultimately transformed into a major telecommunications company, becoming the global leader in mobile phones in the 1990s. In 1992, it launched the first digital mobile phone, the Nokia 1011, and by the end of the year was second only to Motorola in the mobile phone market. The Nokia 3210, launched in 1997, was heralded for its shapely design, interchangeable covers, the availability of different colors, and various ringtones to meet customer preferences. By 1998, Nokia (23% market share) became the first mobile telephone brand to overtake number one Motorola (20% market share).[5]

As described in Chapter 2, while Motorola focused primarily on the traditional technology of its phones, Nokia's strategy was based on digital technology and the technology of design, which appealed to the segment of younger customers who responded favorably to the need for fashion in phones.[6] During its rise to success, Nokia developed a variety of phones and sizes for different countries using the Symbian operating system. As in the case of Motorola and Blackberry discussed in Chapter 4, the launch of Apple's iPhone in 2007 challenged Nokia's dominance. Nokia found it difficult to respond. They managed to maintain a decent global market share into 2010 but largely through selling phones in the low-priced part of the market, which also yielded much lower profit margins than the higher-priced part of the market, dominated by the iPhone.

The emerging imprisonment for Nokia was its continued reliance on the technology driving its Symbian operating system platform. Unfortunately, it was much more difficult for external developers to work with than Apple's iPhone Operating System (IOS) or Google's Android system. In 2010, Nokia's then CEO declared the following: "I have learned that we are standing on a burning platform."[7] The burning platform was of course the Symbian operating system. In 2010, Nokia's app store (then called Ovi) contained 30,000 apps compared to over 300,000 apps in the Apple App Store.[8] The Android Marketplace offered 130,000 apps and RIM had 16,000 apps.[9]

As a step toward remedying the situation in 2011, Nokia abandoned its Symbian platform in favor of an alliance with Microsoft's emerging Windows Mobile Operating System platform. The purpose was to compete with Apple's IOS and Google's Android systems. The continued competitive pressures from Apple and Android phones (Samsung, LG,

HTC, and others) put severe pressure on Nokia's market share and financials. In 2014, Nokia sold its mobile phone business to Microsoft, thus ending a once formidable brand of mobile phones.[10] What went wrong? Why did Nokia hang on to its Symbian operating system in the face of competition?

The Psychic Prison Cell of Fear

A thoughtful and convincing research-based study by Vuori and Huy analyzed the internal organizational life that led to Nokia's loss in the smartphone battle.[11] Their findings were based on validated data from 76 interviews conducted between 2012 and 2014 with Nokia top managers (TopMs), middle managers (MidMs), engineers, and external experts. Their focus was on the downfall between 2005 and 2010. The way in which Nokia was structured at the time involved TopMs who were concerned about the external environment and MidMs who were expected to implement TopM decisions.

The core finding of their research was that the TopMs and MidMs both possessed a fear that created a shared distraction from Nokia's innovation process to meet the Apple iPhone threat. However, their fears were quite different. Nokia's TopMs were very close to the market and surprisingly, knew about Apple's iPhone threat a year before it was launched.[12] Nokia did not have any technology in touchscreens, which greatly concerned the TopMs. This resulted in a high level of concern and fear among the TopMs that they could not meet this competitive threat in a timely manner.

Consequently, in response to this fear, the TopMs reportedly placed a great deal of pressure on the MidMs to develop a competitive product. This in turn resulted in a significant amount of fear among the MidMs. The MidM's fear derived not so much from the external market but from the internal pressures from the TopMs. This occurred in large part because of the reported turbulent organizational environment created by a history of aggressive behaviors of the TopMs against the MidMs.[13] This turned into a relatively high level of fear among MidMs, derived from their negative experiences with TopMs.

The outcome of this situation was a debilitating system of shared fears. TopMs were fearful of aggressive competitors and of shareholders — externally derived fears; the MidMs were fearful of the

TopMs' aggressive behaviors — internally derived fears. As Vuori and Huy concluded from their research:

> In combination, TopMs' external fear and MidMs' internal fear and low external fear produced an interaction pattern between these groups that increased the decoupling between TopMs' and MidMs' perceptions of how quickly Nokia could develop new software and introduce smartphones to match the iPhone... Instead of pushing back, MidMs generally acquiesced to TopMs' demands and continued reporting optimistic progress despite mounting implementation difficulties.[14]

In effect, the MidMs feared communicating a negative message to the TopMs. At this point, both key managerial levels in the organization virtually put themselves into psychic prisons of being incapable of responding to competitive threats.

Misdirected Efforts

The unfortunate circumstance for Nokia was that in order to reach sales targets, the TopMs focused organizational resources on something they were already doing well — developing new hardware. This resulted in less expensive phones aimed at markets that could afford them. This maintained a level of sales for a few years; however, they lost the battle in the operating system software and customer-friendly apps, which were key success factors for the smartphones of the future. Nokia's Symbian system was not up to par with Apple's operating system (iOS) or Google's emerging Android system.

In Morgan's discussion of organizational psychic prisons, anxiety, or fear, is one of the pathologies that contribute to it. It's therefore not surprising that a CEO would pronounce that Nokia was standing on a burning platform — however not the operating system as much as the fears among top and middle managers that placed Nokia in tragic psychic prison cells of fear. This ultimately broke down its brand relationships with current and potential customers. Anxieties and fears among people and units in an organization can create one kind of psychic prison cell that put a brand at risk. There are unfortunately other kinds of prison cells, as will be seen in the case of Kodak.

Kodak: Out of the Picture

From his own need for a lighter and more portable camera to take on a planned vacation trip in 1878, George Eastman, at the age of 24, began working on the technical aspects of photography in his hometown of Rochester, New York.[15] At the time, photography involved the chemistry of developing a gelatin that was placed on sheets of glass for use by photographers who purchased them to take pictures, primarily in studios. In 1883, after numerous experiments, Eastman developed a process to place the gelatin on paper that could be rolled, thus creating rolled film. This innovation led to the development of the first portable Kodak camera (see Figure 7.1):

> With the KODAK Camera in 1888, Eastman put down the foundation for making photography available to everyone. Pre-loaded with enough film for 100 exposures, the camera could be easily carried and handheld during operation. It was priced at $25. After exposure, the whole camera was returned to Rochester. There the film was developed, prints were made, and new film was inserted — all for $10.[16]

Figure 7.1.   Original Kodak Box Camera, 1888

Source: Smithsonian National Museum of American History, https://americanhistory.si.edu/collections/search/object/nmah_760118.

In defining his new camera this way, Eastman created a business model that did not rely on camera hardware sales as much as it did on the service of providing a development process that delivered printed pictures to customers. To implement the process beyond Rochester, Eastman built an ecosystem of retailers (usually drugstores and camera shops) where customers would take their rolls of film for development. The rolls of film were then sent to local and regional firms who developed the pictures, packaged them, and returned them to the retailer for customers to pick up. That business model served Kodak very well for 100 years.

As innovations in photography marched forward, in 1988 Fujifilm announced the FUJIX DS-1P, the world's first truly digital camera. This was an initial signpost for Kodak's troubles ahead. These troubles arrived in a big way during 2001 when several mobile phones were launched with built-in digital cameras. This marked the beginning of Kodak's decline. This was followed in 2007 with the introduction of Apple's iPhone, which put the camera and the development process in the hands of customers. Kodak's business model based on the processing of print pictures was completely at risk. In 2012, Kodak filed for bankruptcy.

Back to the Beginning

It was clear that George Eastman understood the importance of customer needs and engaging customers with compelling advertising communications. The message from these early ad campaigns was "you press the button, we do the rest." The customer came first ("you") in this ad. A customer focus was the first of Eastman's four principles of business. The others were mass production at low cost, worldwide distribution, and extensive advertising.[17] The business model of customers taking a picture and then submitting it to Kodak for processing, which then returned the hard copy printed image to customers, created a connectivity and brand relationship that resulted in one of the strongest brands in the 20th century.

Kodak's first camera in 1888 was the beginning of an aggressive development process that led to many other innovative firsts: the famous lines of Brownie and Instamatic cameras, professional cameras, motion picture film, color photography (Kodachrome and Ektachrome), and digital cameras. Its marketing and communications were exemplary. Ads reminding customers to purchase the Kodak camera included "Open me first" on gift-opening holiday events or the "Kodak moment," a reminder to capture those special events in the lives of customers and their families. Kodak marketing and its ad agencies knew how to communicate effectively to build and maintain its brand connectivity with customers. By 1976, Kodak dominated photography. It accounted for 90% of film sales and 85% of camera sales in America.[18] But then, things began to change.

The Business Model Psychic Prison Cell

In 1975, Kodak engineer Steve Sasson developed the first digital camera — 13 years before Fujifilm announced its FUJIX DS-1P. The FUJIX DS-1P in 1988 was the first camera to save up to 10 photographs of digital data on a semiconductor memory card.[19] Sasson's original Kodak digital camera was a cumbersome product about the size of a 12 inch block of ice that raised more questions and curiosity within the organization than potential opportunity. To take a picture, Sasson would lift the camera up, aim it, take the photo, and then the electronic image would be sent to a television set for viewing. At a 2016 IEEE (Institute of Electrical and Electronics Engineers) award ceremony, Sasson discussed his innovation, how it happened, and the organization's response.[20] In his presentation, he provided observations about why the digital camera was not developed sooner by Kodak.

From one of the slides in his presentation titled "Reaction," his first comment was "Hesitant to demonstrate this concept to highest level of corporate management."[21] As he explained in his talk, the managers to whom he demonstrated the new camera in 1976 were his immediate supervisors and their bosses, primarily middle managers. Their reactions were not about the technology of how it was done but about the fact that it might disrupt the way they conducted their business and the way customers took pictures and had them developed into prints. This was related to the second point on the Reaction slide: "Too far 'out there' for serious consideration."[22] Consequently, as Sasson described it, the highest level and most senior managers in Kodak were not shown the new technology at the time because of the assumption by middle managers that top managers would not see its value in relation to how they currently conducted their business.

Sasson conceded in his talk that they were probably correct — that top-level managers would not respond favorably to the new digital camera. He believed they would see it as a "paradigm shift" that made them uncomfortable. The mindset of senior managers was that there was no real alternative to their business model that would even come close to their current one. As Sasson stated: "They're really smart guys. They're not dumb. They're not arrogant. They didn't miss anything. They just couldn't see the business model that was competing with what they had."[23] What they had was a very profitable ecosystem with printed pictures that created a perfect *business model psychic prison cell* that managers at all levels could not easily escape.

Part of the reason for maintaining its business model was pragmatic. Kodak owned a long-held core competence in print imaging and the ecosystem to support it. This defined its business and path to success for almost 100 years. It knew this better than any competitor. This competence insured its prominent market position and sales and profit performance. Even if it recognized and understood the impact of digital camera technology, if it was going to respond to this, it would have to invest in some kind of online place for customers to store and share photos. Not only would this require a substantial investment to develop but in the 1970s, there were no immanent competitive threats from competitive digital cameras nor reasons to believe customers would change their habits.

The Habituation Psychic Prison Cell

Habits are powerful yet unconscious drivers of behavior, with estimates indicating some "45% of people's behavior is repeated almost daily and usually in the same context."[24] They are tendencies that humans have established from past patterns of behavior to meet their needs. When the need arises, the behavior is almost automatically triggered into action, often without the awareness of the person about the action. Customers have habits, and managers have habits. Managers often make intuitive assumptions about the behavior of their current customer base, habits that have sometimes been entrenched for many years. In so doing, managers themselves engage in the habit of assuming how customers respond to their offers and therefore run the risk of putting themselves in the psychic prison cell of habituation.

As Neale Martin described in the introduction to his book, *Habit*: "This book reveals how two fundamental assumptions have led marketing onto a dead-end path: that customers are aware of what they are doing, and that they know why they do what they do."[25] The same could be said for managers. This was the case for Kodak, which owned the largest market share of cameras and film processing going into 1976. This was also during the time Steven Sasson was showing his digital camera confidentially within Kodak. It was very difficult for managers to imagine how such customer habits might change.

The third point on Sasson's IEEE presentation slide titled "Reactions" was "People won't want to view their images on a TV," an assumption made by managers about the habits of photo customers.[26] The fourth point on his slide was about how customers store images. At the time, they put their photos in an album or kept the pictures in a safe place for occasional viewing. Managers believed that digital storage was simply not a part of the customer's mindset for storing their photos. Of course, they were correct with this assumption at the time, but being entrenched with such managerial habitual thinking made it exceedingly difficult for managers to anticipate and act upon the eventual emergence of digital cameras and phones.

The Rough Road to Bankruptcy

Even with Steven Sasson's digital camera technology in their back pocket, Kodak did not offer a digital camera to the market until they had to respond to severe threats from competitors, such as Fujifilm. During the 1980s, a variety of digital camera patents and innovations emerged from firms such as Sony, Canon, Nikon, Casio, and Olympus putting pressure on Kodak to act. However, it wasn't until the 1988 Fujifilm launch of the FUJIX DS-1P that a full-fledged digital camera with a memory card paved the road to a customer market.[27] Digital photographs without print film became a reality and Kodak had to respond.

Despite its slow start, during the 1980s, Kodak developed the digital camera system (DCS) primarily for government and business applications. This was followed by a stream of digital cameras through the 1990s, including the DC20 and DC25, which were priced lower than professional cameras and targeted at customers. The unfortunate outcome for Kodak's forced evolution into the digital camera arena was that it was not nearly as profitable as its traditional print film business. Furthermore, the fact that customers began to switch to digital from print and that Japanese competitors were taking significant market share made the firm begin to experience considerable financial stress.

In 1993, a new CEO was hired from Motorola: George Fisher. He was the first CEO to be brought in from the outside with the mission to revitalize the organization. He began by refocusing the organization on digital imaging as the future, by addressing financial pressures with debt reduction through the sales of various assets, and by challenging managers to become more action-oriented and growth-focused. He intended to do this by refocusing the organization on the customer, as Kodak's founder once did. However, this was apparently a frustrating task. As noted in a *Business Week* article at the time:

> When Fisher arrived, he found an insular company that venerated authority and frowned on confrontation. "It was so hierarchically oriented that everybody looked to the guy above him for what needed to be done," he says. That led to diffusion of responsibility.[28]

Fisher was experiencing the impact of the psychic prison cells that locked large parts of the management team from responding in a market-focused way. Despite some organizational progress and attempts to improve the business strategically and financially, Kodak remained financially constrained and the organization continued to resist change. As the situation was reported in 1997 in *Business Week*:

> Although he has taken steps to shake things up — such as instituting pay-for-performance standards — the old-line manufacturing culture continues to impede Fisher's efforts to turn Kodak into a high-tech growth company. 'Fisher has been able to change the culture at the very top,' says one industry executive. 'But he hasn't been able to change the huge mass of middle managers, and they just don't understand this [digital] world.'[29]

Fisher's CEO term ended in December 1999, and from 2000 until 2012 when bankruptcy was declared, Kodak and the subsequent CEOs could not overcome its difficulties. The chart in Figure 7.3 shows the stock price rise and fall of Kodak over the years. Ironically, as noted, the initial cost of George Eastman's original camera in 1888 was $35 ($25 for the camera purchase and $10 for development). In 2023 dollars, this would be a price of $1,026 — about the price of a basic iPhone 14 Pro in 2023 ($999), and this did not include the additional $10 costs of developing additional Kodak photos. The sum of competitive challenges, continuing financial difficulty, extensive layoffs, and perhaps most importantly,

Figure 7.3.   50-Year History of Kodak Stock Prices: 1962–2012
Source: Yahoo! Inc. 2012.

an organization locked in psychic prison cells that could not respond to market changes in a timely fashion made bankruptcy the only viable option for Kodak.[30]

Breaking Out of Prison

During the 1990s and going into the 21st century, Nokia in the world of mobile phones and Kodak in the world of photography were among the most popular brands available to customers. Each had strong brand relationships with its customer base. Unfortunately, both brands fell on hard times. As new generations of customers arrive throughout the 21st century, most will never know these brands other than through an occasional reference. Nokia and Kodak are true brand tragedies that in many ways met their downfall because their managers at all levels became locked in organizational psychic prisons. Whether through fear, ongoing business models, habituation, or other psychic prison cells, managers became "trapped by constructions of reality that, at best, give an imperfect grasp on the world."[31] These once great brands were put at risk and ultimately became tragedies.

Once organizational psychic prisons are encountered and understood, there may be a chance to break them. As George Fisher and his successors learned, that was a very difficult if not impossible task. Nevertheless, there are a few practical steps to consider when faced with dire external forces and a strong reluctance to change within the organization: (1) find organizational keys to change and unlock the prison, (2) use data to break habits, and (3) revise strategy.

Find and Legitimize Organizational Keys to Change

Either through outside consultation or internal leadership, identify if the malaise to respond to the need to change is one or more types of psychic prison cells. For example, if fear or anxiety is driving the malaise, seek ways to unlock the prison cell. In such situations, as in the cases of Nokia and Kodak, there are often groups within the organization that argue for change and often have the potential to do so but get no respect or platform for their ideas to be heard. A thoughtful leader can discover, legitimize, and validate this group's ideas to activate the kinds of changes needed.

Use Data to Recognize and Break Habits that Threaten the Brand

Behind every major market change are customers who have established habits of purchasing a brand, which often correlate with managerial rigid habits of relying on customers' continued behavior. However, customer habits can be broken by innovations, competitors, or other changes in the market environment. Inaction because of managerial habit can cost valuable time to respond. An ongoing use of high-quality data to identify segments of customers with changing needs or who respond favorably to changing external factors can provide a pathway to break habits. To be good at this kind of data mining requires an ability to gather data, develop deeper insight into customers, and act.

Progressive firms are using massive amounts of online data and analytics in an insightful way to generate ideas for emerging needs that can be the basis for new market segments. Small but growing segments of customers can often be the harbingers of forthcoming major market changes. Meeting their needs with new products and services and being prepared to scale the firm's ability to do so can provide the data and basis for unlocking the habitual mindset of managers about customer behavior. Wise leaders can break managerial habits and assumptions about customers by refocusing key managers in the organization to understand the importance of market-based data and the centrality of customers to continually reinvigorate the brand.

Innovate, Diversify, and Acquire to Inform Strategic Migrations

In some cases, such as Kodak, a brand's successful business model will inevitably die. As Willy Shih, a senior vice president at Kodak from 1997 to 2003, described, Kodak's business model was clearly not going to survive due to the transition to digital and the management knew it: "senior leaders at Kodak were acutely aware of the approaching storm."[32] Efficiently and effectively downsizing an organization and its manufacturing processes in the face of a declining market is quite difficult under most circumstances. Shih speculated with hindsight that to survive, Kodak might have emulated some actions of its main competitor, Fujifilm. It faced the same business model disruption and difficult market circumstances as Kodak but managed to outlive it with carefully planned strategic migrations.

Fujifilm survived by strategically innovating, diversifying, and acquiring selective companies and technologies. Shigetaka Komori became CEO in 2000 and recognized the difficult situation of traditional photography and developed major survival initiatives.[33] His teams (most likely "agile") generated inventories of all Fujifilm technologies and matched them to potential market opportunities. For example, they used their chemical competency to develop innovative cosmetics, pharmaceuticals, and films for LCD screens. For technologies without clear opportunities, they diversified with acquisition into new markets, such as healthcare. This did not happen overnight. It occurred over a 10-year period as traditional print film sales declined.

Innovation, diversification into new markets, and acquisition take time to develop and digest. They must be accomplished strategically and carefully. Rushing into such ventures without proper data and a strategic view of the markets entered increases risk. Furthermore, not understanding the impact on customers can seriously fragment the brand's relationship with customers and put the brand at risk. Developing a signpost to help recognize when an organization is in, or approaching, a psychic prison or prison cell is another key activity to help identify and possibly avoid brand tragedies. Ideally, leadership can use the three factors in this signpost to take the steps to prevent the occurrence of a psychic prison or escape from it.

Propositions to Consider in Developing a Signpost for Psychic Prisons

The three factors considered above can help develop a signpost for psychic prisons in organizations. While each is briefly summarized here as a proposition, taken together, they require strong leadership to discover, plan, and implement:

- **Find and Legitimize Organizational Keys to Change:** The more difficult to find keys to change, the greater the vulnerability to a brand tragedy.
- **Use Data to Recognize and Break Habits that Threaten the Brand:** The weaker the ability to use data to change organizational habits, the greater the vulnerability to a brand tragedy.
- **Innovate, Diversify, and Acquire to Inform Strategic Migrations:** The more difficult to innovate, diversify, and acquire, the greater the vulnerability to a brand tragedy.

What remains are the steps necessary to manage and rebuild brand relationships with customers that have succumbed to difficult circumstances, whether through technology myopia, ruptured loyalties, bruising viral spirals, catastrophes, broken leadership, psychic prisons, or some combination of these factors. Using these factors as initial signposts for tragedies may provide a way to preempt or confront impending challenges to the brand. This will be the primary focus of Chapter 8.

Endnotes

1. Morgan, Gareth, *Images of Organization*. Newbury Park, CA: Sage Publications, 1986.
2. *Ibid.*, p. 219.
3. Thomas, Robert J., *New Product Development: Managing and Forecasting for Strategic Success*. New York: John Wiley & Sons, 1993, p. 80.
4. Yoder, Stephen K., "Motorola Loses Edge in Microprocessors by Delaying New Chips," *The Wall Street Journal*, March 4, 1991, 1+.

5. Gartner, "Mobile Phone Vendor's Market Share in Sold Units to End Users Worldwide from 1997 to 2014." *Chart*. March 3, 2015. *Statista*. Accessed August 7, 2019. https://www-statista-com.proxy.library. georgetown.edu/statistics/271574/global-market-share-held-by-mobile-phone-manufacturers-since-2009/.

6. Oremus, Will, "When Cellphones Became Cool," *Slate*, September 20, 2016. https://slate.com/technology/2016/09/the-development-of-the-nokia-3210-the-cellphone-that-started-the-mobile-revolution. html (Accessed May 24, 2022).

7. Siegler, Chris, "Nokia CEO Stephen Elop Rallies Troops in Brutally Honest 'Burning Platform' Memo? (Update: It's Real!)," *Engadget. com*, February 8, 2011. https://www.engadget.com/2011-02-08-nokia-ceo-stephen-elop-rallies-troops-in-brutally-honest-burnin.html (Accessed May 24, 2022).

8. Jahns, Ralph-Gordon, "6 Major Trends Shaping the Smartphone App Ecosystem in 2010," *Research2Guidance*, October 4, 2010, https:// research2guidance.com/6-major-trends-shaping-the-smartphone-app-ecosystem-in-2010-2/ (Accessed May 24, 2022).

9. "Nokia Ovi Store app total tops 30,000," *Mobile World Live*, January 31, 2011, https://www.mobileworldlive.com/apps/news-apps/nokia-ovi-store-app-total-tops-30-000/ (Accessed May 24, 2022).

10. Cooper, Daniel, "The Collapse of Microsoft and Nokia's Mobile Business," *Engadget.com*, April 22, 2016. https://www.engadget. com/2016/04/22/microsoft-mobile-timeline/ (Accessed May 24, 2022).

11. Vuori, Timo O. and Quy N. Huy, "Distributed Attention and Shared Emotions in the Innovation Process: How Nokia Lost the Smartphone Battle," *Administrative Science Quarterly*, March 2016, 61(1), 9–51.

12. Vuori and Huy, *Op. cit.*, p. 22.

13. *Ibid.*, p. 24.

14. *Ibid.*, p. 30.

15. See Kodak corporate website for historical details: https://www. kodak.com/en/company/page/george-eastman-history (Accessed April 4, 2023).

16. *Ibid*.

17. *Ibid*.

18. Gavetti, Giovanni, Rebecca Henderson, Simona Giorgi, *Kodak and the Digital Revolution (A)*. Case 9-705-448, Boston, MA: Harvard Business School Publishing, November 2, 2005.

19. Wikipedia contributors, "Digital camera," *Wikipedia, The Free Encyclopedia.* https://en.wikipedia.org/w/index.php?title=Digital_camera&oldid=1146129218 (Accessed April 4, 2023).

20. Sasson, Steven J., "2016 IEEE Masaru Ibuka Consumer Electronics Award," published on February 17, 2016, https://www.youtube.com/watch?v=4Qh08tiXzhA (Accessed May 24, 2022).

21. *Ibid.*

22. *Ibid.*

23. *Ibid.*

24. Wood, Wendy and David T. Neal, "The Habitual Consumer," *Journal of Consumer Psychology*, 19, 2009, 579–592, 579.

25. Martin, Neale, *Habit: The 95% of Behavior Marketers Ignore.* Upper Saddle River, NJ: New Jersey FT Press, 2010, p. xv.

26. Sasson, *Op. cit.*

27. For a history of digital cameras see the following website: The Digital Camera Museum, https://www.digitalkameramuseum.de/en/history (Accessed May 24, 2022).

28. Maremont, Mark, "Kodak's New Focus," *Bloomberg Business Week*, January 30, 1995. https://www.bloomberg.com/news/articles/1995-01-29/kodaks-new-focus (Accessed May 24, 2022).

29. Smith, Geoffrey, "Can George Fisher Fix Kodak?" *Bloomberg Business Week*, October 20, 1997. https://www.bloomberg.com/news/articles/1997-10-19/can-george-fisher-fix-kodak (Accessed May 24, 2022).

30. For a summary of the business and financial aspects of the Kodak situation, see Gavetti, *et al., Op. cit.*

31. Morgan, *Op. cit.*, p. 216.

32. Shih, Willy, "The Real Lessons From Kodak's Decline," *MIT Sloan Management Review*, 57(4), Summer 2016, 19–22.

33. For a summary of the comparison of the two companies, see: Kmia, Oliver, "Why Kodak Died and Fujifilm Thrived: A Tale of Two Film Companies," *PetaPixel.com*, October 19, 2018. https://petapixel.com/2018/10/19/why-kodak-died-and-fujifilm-thrived-a-tale-of-two-film-companies/ (Accessed May 24, 2022).

Chapter 8

How Leaders Can Manage Threats to Brand Equity

The world has seen its share of brand tragedies. Haig describes 100 in his book[1] and CB Insights cataloged 160 new product brand failures,[2] many of which are from well-known national brands. While organizations are destined to have failures, especially for new products, this book has been concerned with how the leadership of successful brands encounter a potentially tragic situation and take actions to resolve it ... or not.

Do leaders who experience a brand-threatening situation accelerate into a real tragedy or do they find a way to avoid it? In this final chapter, a process is outlined that suggests steps to better anticipate and manage a potentially tragic brand situation. The objective is to defend, maintain, and even build, a brand's equity for the organization, its customers, and other stakeholders.

The proposed process may not work for every organization or brand tragedy, but it is one that suggests a comprehensive way forward for thoughtful leaders and managers who truly care about their brands, their customers, their organization, and their stakeholders. The process, with five major phases, includes consideration of the six signposts for tragedies to inform the development of a Brand Tragedy Index. The process can be used to prepare for a brand tragedy and to develop a response for one that has occurred:

- *Phase One*: Build a brand tragedy response team
- *Phase Two*: Understand the brand's history

- *Phase Three*: Prepare for brand tragedies with a Brand Tragedy Index
- *Phase Four*: Design remedial options
- *Phase Five*: Execute and monitor customer response

While each of these sets of activities is briefly considered in the following sections, the actual implementation of the process can involve far more study and analysis than space permits in a book chapter. The phases are also interactive, requiring a sensitivity to continuously review and update previous phases to pursue a current phase most effectively. In addition, due to the variability in organizations, customers, and their brand relationships, the process may be structured and implemented differently according to each situation.

Phase One: Build a Brand Tragedy Response Team

The value of a leader creating a collaborative and agile team to prepare for and possibly work on a brand tragedy cannot be underestimated. The purpose of a team is for its participants to work together to achieve objectives and goals. This is not the place for a full discussion of teamwork, however the work by Hackman[3] describes several important conditions that can lead to collaborative teamwork effectiveness. For a real team to succeed, it must have a compelling team purpose with the right people on the team. Clear norms of conduct and organizational support for teamwork are also essential, as is well-timed team coaching.

It is also important for teams to be flexible and agile, especially in response to turbulent environments that can create a brand tragedy. Recognizing the need for sub-teams with sub-goals may complicate the process, but applying the same basic rules for teamwork to the sub-teams will also improve their effectiveness.

The people to place on such a team should be involved in the normal management of the brand. Ideally, such a team would be appointed and led by the CEO. Key functions on the team might typically include marketing (product management, sales, and communication), operations, information technology, product development (including R&D), human resources, and finance. It is also vitally important to recognize that when dealing with brand tragedies, the team may not succeed in achieving its goals. While every organization's culture may vary with regard to dealing with failures, the organization and everyone on the team should recognize and be prepared for such outcomes.

Phase Two: Understand the Brand's History

As philosopher George Santayana is often quoted: "Those who cannot remember the past are condemned to repeat it." Understanding a brand's history is the stepping stone to anticipating and recovering from a tragic breakdown in the brand's relationship with customers. If the history of an important brand is not deeply understood, then it is imperative to conduct the necessary research to learn it, write it, and communicate it to relevant stakeholders — and this should not happen *after* a tragedy but *before* it in order to be prepared when one occurs.

It is surprising how many books about brand strategy neglect the importance of knowing and understanding a brand's history, especially as it relates to building brand relationships. An example of written brand history for the Tata brand is provided by Morgen Witzel.[4] It's an example of how understanding the history of a brand in terms of its founder's values helped uncover why customers were attracted to it and established its real value as a brand — even to withstand product failures. Witzel tells the story of Tata, named after its founder, Jamsetji N. Tata, which eventually becomes a global industrial conglomerate in India with numerous sub-brands all beginning with the core brand of Tata. Tata Motors, Tata Steel, Tata Tea, Tata Power, Tata Communications, and others all share the core values of its founder to create a strong brand value foundation for its customers and its firm.

The following quote by the founder, Jamsetji N. Tata, reveals the value-driven purpose of his organization: "In a free enterprise, the community is not just another stakeholder in business, but is in fact, the very purpose of its existence."[5] Five core values drive their business and brands. They include integrity, responsibility, excellence, pioneering, and unity. Even when its much-touted Tata Nano car brand failed, the Tata Motors brand continued to thrive.

The book about Tata is one example of many ways to implement a historical analysis of a brand. It requires an analyst or other interested party who studies the company and draws insights and conclusions about the brand and its history. A more generalized approach recommended by Sager and Rosser[6] helps define methodical steps for a proper historical inquiry. Slightly adapted here, these steps outline a research process and include the following: (1) define the brand in focus, (2) identify sources of brand-relevant information, (3) collect, analyze, and validate the information, (4) draw inferences to tell the brand history, and (5) communicate the brand history to the organization. Each step is briefly considered.

(1) Define the Brand in Focus: Recalling from Chapter 1, a brand was defined as a name or mark assigned to an entity for identification. In the context of defining a brand's history for many organizations, it begins with identifying the company's brand architecture and the specific brand in focus.[7] In its simplest form, it can be a single brand name that defines a number of products or services or even an entire company. For example, the brand Gorilla Glue is the name of the company and the core brand for some 27 product variations of glue and adhesives, 15 tape products, and five sealant products. A history of the "Gorilla" brand would be the proper focus.

At the other extreme of brand definition are firms with a corporate name and numerous brands within it. Consider Beiersdorf (the name of the founder and the company). It has numerous brands in the skincare field, including NIVEA, Eucerin, La Prairie, Labello, and Coppertone. The history of the Beiersdorf company is of course interesting,[8] however the history of a specific brand in focus, such as NIVEA, may be more relevant to understanding the brand and its relationship with customers. Consequently, this first step in the historical analysis is to have a clearly defined brand unit of analysis in focus.

(2) Identify Sources of Brand Relevant Information: Understanding a brand's history requires a serious and sometimes challenging effort to conduct research using various sources of information. Figure 8.1 provides a variety of suggested information sources to consider, which may depend on a brand organization's business and markets. A treasure trove of valuable information is often found in a variety of **company** sources, especially those related to the founder's records and other internal documents. Brand founders will often write a book based on their own history of the brand, as was the case with Alan Wurtzel, son of Circuit City's founder. Other sources include those from a variety of published media, social media, academic journals, research reports, and books.

Recall that the core meaning and value of a brand are derived from its **customers**. Obtaining customer information is perhaps the most important source of insights about a brand and its market. Information from marketing research studies, customer visits, and a variety of online and other data sources will help reveal why the brand succeeds or not with customers. If a firm does not have one, it is essential to build a customer playbook that defines the overall customer journey, among other factors. It should include customer needs and problems, sources of information they use,

Company	Customers	Collaborators	Competitors
Founder records	Market research	Suppliers	Industry reports
Websites	Customer visits	Wholesalers	Websites
Marketing promotions	Social media	Retailers	Marketing promotions
Press releases	Company websites	Subcontractors	Press releases
Employee records	Purchase histories	Consultants	Speeches/Articles
Speeches/Articles	Customer complaints	Industry associations	Patents
Patents/White papers	Customer returns	Security analyst reports	Annual reports
Annual reports	Industry reports	Government documents	Lawsuits
Other...	Other...	Other....	Other...

Figure 8.1.   Potential Sources of Historical Brand Information with Examples

competitive options considered to meet the needs, how they compare and evaluate different brands, how and why they choose a brand, how they use it, and the extent to which they communicate with others about it.

Various sources of external market **collaborators** involved in delivering customer value as listed in Figure 8.1 can also open insights into a brand's history. To the extent it is available, information about **competitors** can uncover useful insights about a brand and its history. The value of information sources about a brand, such as proposed in Figure 8.1, is that multiple views are obtained from different market stakeholders, not just a company's own view. Having multiple sources also helps manage the natural biases that may accompany the information derived from each one.

(3) Collect, Analyze, and Validate the Brand Information: Perhaps the most crucial step in establishing a reasonably accurate brand history is collecting, analyzing, and validating the information from the various sources identified. The process is far more complex than can be described in this chapter and varies considerably by organization in terms of the sources of data and database management system employed.[9]

In terms of data collection, internally stored legacy data may be found and accessed in flat files or relational databases. Past marketing research studies are an example. Data from external sources will often include those from social media and other online sites. Working with information technology and database experts in the brand's organization, as well as external vendors, may be essential to collecting the data necessary for historical analysis.

Some data may be collected as *numbers* and possibly analyzed with statistical techniques and modeling. Substantial *text* data may be analyzed with the various human and emerging automated analytic approaches. Tracking a brand's sales performance over time is an example of numeric data, whereas statements about a brand from an annual report or a social media site represent text data. Whatever way the data are analyzed, to the extent possible, the concepts and measurement approaches should be fact-checked and validated, both internally and externally.

(4) Draw Inferences to Tell the Brand History: At its core, a brand's history is a story with a setting and characters (often one or more founders). It is a narrative with a beginning, a middle, and an end. The story is derived from information collected, analyzed, and validated from the previous phase. The origin of a brand's story may vary considerably, but many often begin with a customer's problem. It can be a founder, a team of researchers, or managers who study the possible options to solve the problem and build a potential solution. It is their journey to the solution and coupling it with the brand that makes up the middle part of the story. The final part of the story is the performance of the brand with customers.

Holt provides a good example of how the process works in the context of studying a brand's history, or "genealogy" through customer communications, and drawing inferences from it.[10] He describes how to build a chronological interpretation of the content of a brand by studying the history of its advertisements. By reviewing the elements of an ad over time and associating it with a chronology of culture during the same period, he establishes the cultural meaning of a brand's position in the environment of social, political, and economic factors.

Holt's process starts with a firm's own managerial interpretation of the effectiveness of its advertising — why they believe some ads resonated with customers and some didn't. The process continues by linking the ad effects to parallel cultural and social changes. This kind of time-based analysis of a brand's communication enables the development of a resonating story to explain the historical significance of the brand in culture, more so than in the context of the organization. While Holt uses his genealogical method to develop theory, it also illustrates a comprehensive path to building the history of a brand. In his book, he provides examples of histories of brands including Budweiser, VW, Nike, and ESPN (sports network).

(5) Communicate the Brand History to the Organization: Preparing a brand's history is one thing; effectively communicating it to appropriate audiences is quite another. Iglesias and colleagues[11] make the case for studying the history of an organization's business, strategy, and brand, especially one that may be experiencing a difficult situation and need revitalization. They briefly describe the market and financial plight of Adidas associated with a leadership team that pursued a strategy of brand extensions that diluted the brand's core value. By pursuing a deep study of the origins of the brand and the values of its founder, Adi Dassler, they were able to return to a set of core values that led to innovation and a resuscitation of the brand.

The process they recommend for communicating a brand's history once uncovered and brought into focus involves managers promoting the organizational structures and processes that help history to be remembered, promoting the curation of history in order to make it relevant for the current context, and embedding history to support future strategy. The benefits of studying and uncovering a brand's history are many, including humanizing and authenticating it, inspiring future strategies for it, motivating change when needed, and most relevant in the case of tragedies, assisting in understanding brand relationships with customers that have broken down. In most organizations, the involvement of their internal educational, training, and communication capabilities will be needed to support the effective communication of a brand's history.

Phase Three: Prepare for Brand Tragedies with a Brand Tragedy Index

As often quoted by Benjamin Franklin: "By failing to prepare, you are preparing to fail." You don't know when a tragedy may befall your brand. However, considering the use of the fundamental signposts developed in the last six chapters can help prepare an organization to better identify the early onset of a tragedy or help diagnose one that is occurring. While different firms may take different approaches to prepare for difficult market situations, a Brand Tragedy Index (BTI) is proposed as a methodology to stimulate thinking and preparation for a difficult situation involving the brand.

The fundamental idea is to develop a measurement approach using the concept of a brand's "vulnerability," which is defined as the exposure to the possibility of a tragedy. Using various measurement approaches, a BTI can be quantified to help estimate a brand's vulnerability to a tragedy. Generally, the higher the value of a BTI, the greater the likelihood of a potential tragedy. Three levels of measurement are considered: (1) a global estimate, (2) one based on the six signposts, and (3) a more comprehensive estimate based on the six signposts and three factors for each.

(1) Global Estimation of the Brand Tragedy Index: The most basic estimate of the BTI is to ask selected organizational leaders and managers to answer a "global" question about the likelihood of a tragedy occurring for their brand. By collecting the individual and averaged beliefs of this selected team, a very rough estimate of the potential for a brand tragedy can be obtained. The importance and composition of this team were discussed in Phase One of this process. The global question can be phrased and measured as follows:

> How would you rate the overall vulnerability of your brand to a serious tragedy of any kind?

An 11-point rating scale can be used in which the value of zero means "Not At All Vulnerable" up to the value of 10 which means "Extremely Vulnerable." See Figure 8.2 for an example of such a global measurement scale.

(2) Six Signposts Estimation of the Brand Tragedy Index: As developed in the last six chapters, the six signposts can be used to construct a more informed BTI. This involves constructing a rating scale similar to the global one presented in the previous section. This provides a somewhat more refined estimate of the BTI than the global one. As in the previous

How would you rate the overall vulnerability of your brand to a serious tragedy of any kind?										
Not At All Vulnerable									Extremely Vulnerable	
0	1	2	3	4	5	6	7	8	9	10

Figure 8.2.   Global Estimation of the Brand Tragedy Index

Please carefully read each of the following statements about how vulnerable your brand may be to a tragedy and provide a rating based on your current beliefs using the scale provided.	Not At All Vulnerable									Extremely Vulnerable
1. How vulnerable is your brand to Technology Myopia? The ability to anticipate the velocity, variety, and visibility of new technologies that impact our brand.	0	1	2	3	4	5	6	7	8	(9)	10
2. How vulnerable is your brand to Ruptured Loyalties? The ability of your firm's key leaders and managers to think, feel, and behave in a loyal manner to their customers.	0	1	2	3	(4)	5	6	7	8	9	10
3. How vulnerable is your brand to Bruising Viral Spirals? The ability to understand the viral dynamics of a market, preparation to respond to a viral situation, and engage virally with market stakeholders.	0	1	(2)	3	4	5	6	7	8	9	10
4. How vulnerable is your brand to Catastrophes? The ability to frame an immediate strategic response, conduct a proper systems analysis of the situation, and rebuild trust with customers.	0	1	2	3	4	(5)	6	7	8	9	10
5. How vulnerable is your brand to Leadership Lost? The inadequacy of leadership to maintain closeness with customers, run strategically agile organizations, and support smooth leadership transitions.	0	1	2	3	4	5	6	7	8	9	(10)
6. How vulnerable is your brand to a Psychic Prison? The presence of strong organizational habitual behaviors that prevent behavioral change, dismiss data to identify new opportunities, and delay strategic innovation?	0	1	2	3	4	5	6	7	8	9	(10)
Summary Vulnerability Score (Average of Six Vulnerabilities)								6.7		

Figure 8.3.   Six Signposts Estimation of the Brand Tragedy Index

BTI, the response team and selected other experts can be asked to provide their estimates of brand vulnerability with the following introduction:

> Please carefully read each of the following statements about how vulnerable your brand may be to a serious tragedy and provide a rating based on your current beliefs using the scale provided.

Similar to the global estimate of BTI, an 11-point rating scale can be used in which the value of zero means "Not At All Vulnerable" up to value of 10 which means "Extremely Vulnerable." See Figure 8.3 for an example of this signpost.

The signpost scale improves upon the global measurement scale by providing more detailed descriptions of the potential sources of a brand tragedy. Also, organizations can modify the six signposts according to their specific markets or brand situations, including adding or deleting signposts. Using the six separate scores, a summary index can be developed based on the simple mean score of the six signpost ratings. As shown in Figure 8.3, a summary value of 6.7 indicates possible vulnerabilities. Closer inspection of the BTI of 6.7 reveals three of the six signposts that may put the brand at risk: technology myopia, leadership lost and a psychic prison mindset.

It is also possible to estimate an importance weight for each of the six signposts and multiply the rating for each signpost by the importance weight. By summing all the weighted scores, a weighted BTI based on the six signposts can be estimated. This weighting procedure is illustrated in the next measurement approach.

(3) Comprehensive Signpost Estimation of the Brand Tragedy Index:
The comprehensive signpost estimate of the BTI is based on the six signposts and the three factors for each one. Each of the 18 factors is presented as a more detailed proposition about a brand's vulnerability to a tragedy. These propositions were developed in Chapters 2 through 7. Using an 11-point rating scale, like the ones presented for the previous two BTI ratings, key leaders and managers involved can estimate a more comprehensive measure of vulnerability for each factor. The construction of the BTI is shown in detail in Figure 8.4.

To illustrate the use of this more comprehensive signpost estimation process, consider the first signpost of technology myopia. As discussed in Chapter 2, the technology that supports a brand may be complex in its structure. This can include software coding or complex electrical and mechanical machines and devices. For many reasons, the people who manage the brand and all its dimensions may not see an oncoming technology that is relevant to a brand's value, thereby putting the brand at risk with competitors and customers. Furthermore, the brand may be comprised of so many different technologies and components that it becomes difficult to anticipate the arrival of threats from any one or more of these technologies.

The core question for this signpost involves the brand's vulnerability to the multiple dimensions of a technology. Recall from Chapter 2 the three key factors identified that may be the source of this myopia: velocity, variety, and visibility. Each is restated in the following as a general proposition identifying potential vulnerability for a brand tragedy.

- **Velocity:** The greater the *velocity* of technology change in a market, the greater the vulnerability to a brand tragedy.

Summary of vulnerability signposts and propositions threatening a brand's success and equity	Factor Weight X	Vulnerability Rating	Weighted Score
1. Technology Myopia Signpost Factors	●————————▶		8.2
Velocity: The greater the velocity of technology change in a market, the greater the vulnerability.	20%	8	1.6
Variety: The greater the variety of new technologies influencing a market, the greater the vulnerability.	30%	7	2.1
Visibility: The less visibility of new and relevant technologies in a market, the greater the vulnerability.	50%	9	4.5
2. Ruptured Loyalties Signpost Factors	●————————▶		3.5
Cognitive: The weaker a firm's ability to *think* about their loyalty to customers, the greater the vulnerability.	40%	2	0.8
Affective: The weaker a firm's ability to *feel* their loyalty to customers, the greater the vulnerability.	30%	4	1.2
Behavioral: The weaker a firm's ability to *behave* loyally to customers, the greater the vulnerability.	30%	5	1.5
3. Bruising Viral Spirals Signpost Factors	●————————▶		1.6
Viral Market Dynamics: The greater the viral dynamics in a market, the greater the vulnerability.	50%	0	0.0
Viral Response Planning: The weaker the viral response planning, the greater the vulnerability.	20%	2	0.4
Viral Engagement: The less prepared brand providers are to engage virally, the greater the vulnerability.	30%	4	1.2
4. Catastrophe Signpost Factors	●————————▶		4.8
Response Quality: The more difficult to frame an immediate strategic response, the greater the vulnerability.	40%	4	1.6
Systems Analytics: The more difficult to conduct a proper systems analysis, the greater the vulnerability.	20%	6	1.2
Trust Rebuilding: The more difficult to rebuild customer trust, the greater the vulnerability.	40%	5	2.0
5. Leadership Lost Signpost Factors	●————————▶		9.5
Customer Distance: The greater the physical distance between leaders & customers, the greater the vulnerability.	50%	9	4.5
Strategic Agility: The less capable leaders are to build agile organizations, the greater the vulnerability.	30%	10	3.0
Leadership Transition: The weaker the orchestration of leadership transitions, the greater the vulnerability.	20%	10	2.0
6. Psychic Prison Signpost Factors	●————————▶		9.8
Organizational Change: The more difficult to identify keys to change, the greater the vulnerability.	10%	10	1.0
Data Mining: The weaker the ability to use data to change organizational habits, the greater the vulnerability.	20%	9	1.8
Strategic Migrations: The more difficult to innovate, diversify, and acquire, the greater the vulnerability.	70%	10	7.0
Overall Brand Tragedy Index Score			6.2

Figure 8.4.   Comprehensive Signpost Estimation of the Brand Tragedy Index

- **Variety:** The greater the *variety* of new technologies that influence a market, the greater the vulnerability to a brand tragedy.
- **Visibility:** The less *visibility* of new and relevant technologies in a market, the greater the vulnerability to a brand tragedy.

To describe the construction of the BTI for this first signpost of technology myopia, consider the second row of the table in Figure 8.4 labeled as follows: 1. *Technology Myopia Signpost Factors.* The next three rows include each of the three factors with a brief statement of the proposition as a reminder. The last three columns of the table are labeled "Factor Weight," "Vulnerability Score," and "Weighted Score." The Factor Weight is based on a constant-sum scale to estimate the relative importance of each of the three factors. The scale varies from zero to 100%. If all three factors were equally important, then each would receive a weight of 33.33%. In Figure 8.4, the three factors were assessed to be 20%, 30%, and 50% respectively in relative importance as sources of a brand's vulnerability.

The second column of the table includes the brand's vulnerability score on that specific factor. It is identical in structure to the previous BTI estimation using the rating scale from 0 to 10 (where 0=Not At All Vulnerable to 10=Extremely Vulnerable). Each of the three factors is then rated in terms of their assessed vulnerability. In this case, the rating for each is 8, 7, and 9, respectively.

The third and final column of the table includes the Weighted Average for each signpost factor. This is simply the product of the Factor Weight times the Vulnerability Score for each signpost factor. In the technology myopia case, the summary score for each is 1.6, 2.1, and 4.5, respectively. The overall signpost vulnerability score is then obtained by summing these three factor weights. This will provide a value from 0 to 10, which can then be considered with the other five signposts. In Figure 8.4, this value is shown as 8.2 on a 10-point scale. This score is located above the three factors in the gray shaded area with the long arrow pointing to the value.

The estimation process can then be completed for the six signposts and each of the three factors as shown in Figure 8.4. Finally, all six summary signpost scores can be averaged to provide an overall BTI estimate. This value (6.2 in this case) is shown in the last row in Figure 8.4. It is simply the mean score of each of the six signpost factors. This more comprehensive estimate of the BTI provides diagnostic opportunities to identify areas of strength and weakness. While these BTI estimates are summarized as numbers that can reveal potential brand vulnerabilities (and strengths), how the various BTI indices can be used in practice is important to consider.

(4) Using the Brand Tragedy Index: As noted in Phase One of this process, using the Brand Tragedy Index (BTI) begins with the brand tragedy response team. There are a variety of ways in which various estimates for a BTI can be developed. For example, a simple arithmetic average or mean score from the various rating scales would provide a basic BTI. However, the mean score does not reflect the distribution of responses across the response team, which may include valuable insights. Consequently, a more rigorous approach, such as the Delphi methodology, is recommended to arrive at a more informed estimate of the BTI.[12] Using it assumes a variety of data has been collected as described in Phases Two and Three, which includes understanding the brand's history and its customers. It also assumes that all members of the response team have reviewed this information.

The objective of the Delphi process involves a group of experts (the response team in this case) arriving at consensus judgments of the BTI based on the independent estimates from each person on the response team. It is also possible to include others in this process if their expertise and insights are relevant. The process begins with the first round of independent estimates (in-person or virtually) of the BTI being considered. The entire team convenes and then reviews the distribution of estimates. After discussion of these estimates, the team is asked to conduct another round of independent estimates. Again, the distribution of responses is shared with the entire group and another discussion prevails. At this point, the team may decide that a consensus BTI estimate has been obtained or they may opt for another round of discussion until a consensus is reached.

The use of the Delphi methodology or any other approach to obtain BTI estimates requires a decision about which of the three estimation processes to use. The most basic is the Global BTI estimation process using a single 11-point scale. It may be most useful in situations where the brand team simply requires some basic thought be given to the possibility of a brand tragedy as measured by its overall vulnerability. In other cases, a brand response team may want a more nuanced BTI measure based on the six signposts or other identified signposts. Again, the Delphi approach may be considered, but in this case, six different estimates will be required. If a more comprehensive BTI estimate is required, the Delphi methodology will likely become cumbersome to use. Alternatively, simple averages of ratings by the response team can be used or specified subteams of experts can be used to obtain Delphi estimates of each set of factors.

Like any index, the usefulness of the BTI may best be realized when its numerical values are understood and tracked over time. For example, in the simplest case of a 12-person brand response team, the mean score is important but so too are other measures of central tendency, such as the median and the mode. In addition, reviewing the actual distribution of responses and measures of dispersion (e.g., range, standard deviation, and variance) can provide insights into areas requiring additional diagnosis and discussion.

Ideally, the use of a BTI with benchmarks over time or compared to competitors can be developed. The interpretation of the numeric values can also vary. For example, a score of 4.1 on an 11-point scale can be an absolute index number or it can be converted to a percent, e.g., 41%. It is also useful as a diagnostic tool with the six signposts and 18 factors before a tragedy occurs to spot corrective actions and possibly at the very beginning of a tragedy to develop appropriate responses. The patterns of high and low risks of occurrences can help direct attention to identify areas of improvement and resource allocation.

While a well-constructed BTI can be obtained, care should be taken in its use. For example, when using a BTI index based on the six signposts, it should be recognized that the six factors are not independent of each other. They are somewhat correlated, especially with regard to topics of leadership and responses to the various factors driving a tragedy. It is also important to recognize that the BTI is not based on any scientific or theoretical foundation rather it is simply a managerial tool based on the logic of the potential for brand tragedies that can occur and possible remediations as reviewed throughout the book. In practice, an organization should consider its own set of signposts and factors as a basis for anticipating and responding to a brand tragedy.

In summary, the BTI provides an opportunity for organizations to think through the potential sources of brand tragedies and their vulnerability to one occurring. It can be another indicator in a brand's dashboard of key metrics (e.g., awareness, trial, and usage). The example of the six

signposts and the factors used here are merely suggestive of other possibilities. Additional signposts and factors for each can be developed.

Phase Four: Design Remedial Options

There is no single remedial option or course of action that may be right
for any specific brand tragedy. It is a matter of experience, judgment, and
creativity of the people involved in the situation. As discussed in the
preceding three phases of the process, knowing the brand's history and
brand relationships with customers are important steps in the process.
Ultimately, the most important process phase may be using the information provided by the Brand Tragedy Index as a basis for generating remedial options.

For example, the overall Brand Tragedy Index of 6.2 indicated in
Figure 8.4 can be interpreted that the brand faces a 62% vulnerability to a
tragedy. This is driven by the high likelihood that the brand's leadership
is at risk (9.5), that the organization suffers from a psychic prison behavioral pattern (9.8), and that it faces vulnerability from a variety of technology factors (8.2). The brand appears to be less vulnerable to demonstrating
loyalty to customers (3.5), experiencing bruising viral spirals (1.6), or
being exposed to catastrophes (4.8). Faced with the higher vulnerabilities,
the organization should develop plans to better cope with the variety, volume, and visibility of technology, although this will be complicated by
organizational leadership issues, which should become a priority to carefully evaluate in this case.

Practically, organizational change during a tragedy may not be immediately possible, which highlights the need for anticipating and planning
for a tragedy. This brief hypothetical scenario based on Figure 8.4 also
suggests the importance of developing the BTI before a tragedy occurs.
Identifying the specific risk factors from a BTI such as this may help
frame the areas requiring remedial action but does not specify the remedial options. This requires both analysis and creativity.

The key to developing remedial options is based on simulating the
possible responses to different kinds of tragic scenarios and constructing
specific actions to be taken. There are many ways to achieve creative possibilities, including the ever-popular brainstorming,[13] synectics[14] (combin-
ing diverse elements of a problem), or lateral thinking.[15] Whichever way
an organization uses to creatively define options, the desired outcome is

to develop scenarios for courses of action to respond to a current or potential brand tragedy.

Phase Five: Execute and Monitor Customer Response

Every firm has its own process for executing and monitoring responses to its actions. Two important dimensions of this process for brand leaders are presented as reminders: adhere to a discipline of execution and recognize the complexity of responding to a tragedy by using checklists.

(1) Adhere to a Discipline of Execution: Covey, McChesney, and Huling offer four key disciplines of execution briefly summarized here.[16] (1) Focus on a few (2–3) wildly important goals because there are more good ideas than the ability to execute them all, i.e., focus on less to achieve more. (2) Act on the lead measures that provide the most leverage to achieve goals, e.g., increasing the number of customers aware of a brand (lead measure) can increase sales (lag measure). (3) Keep a compelling scoreboard; a simple scoreboard of lead measures can activate people to engage in actions more than without one. (4) Create a cadence of accountability that holds team members accountable for their actions; meet weekly or as needed to decide the next steps. This discipline is critical for execution and fortunately not difficult to follow. The team working on the brand tragedy must understand the key steps and their importance to achieving their ultimate goal.

(2) Use Checklists for Complex Tasks: Gawande provides an excellent argument and evidence for developing and using checklists, especially for complex tasks.[17] This is clearly the case for many brand tragedies. A checklist is essentially a tool that aids in developing higher standards of enforcement to protect against failure during implementation. Checklists can be used to review tasks that have been completed to identify if anything has not been completed (Do-Confirm checklists) or to do a task, check it off the list, and then go to the next one

(Read-Do checklists). The most effective checklists tend to have five to nine items.

In the case of potential brand tragedies, each one may require a different checklist. Nevertheless, the Signposts in Figure 8.4 can provide a starting point if considered as a 6-point checklist. Each signpost can have sub-checklists depending on the complexity of the situation. In any case, the use of checklists is strongly recommended especially when the potential risks of harm are evident. Gawande provides guidelines for the development, drafting, and validation of checklists in his book. This is a good starting point for any situation with complexity and important outcomes.[18]

Going Forward

The message should be clear for any brand providers that desire a positive future for their brand — always do your best to take actions that address vulnerabilities associated with the six signposts proposed: technology myopia, ruptured loyalties, bruising viral spirals, catastrophes, leadership lost, and psychic prisons. Any one or more of these potential sources of tragedy can occur and as described in each chapter, can permanently or temporarily destroy a brand.

The rise and fall of brands considered in these chapters should provide sufficient concern to brand providers that the road ahead is not always a smooth one. No matter how successful a brand's performance is, tragedy may be around the corner. The five-phase process proposed in this chapter provides a rough set of guidelines to help anticipate and respond to a brand tragedy. Rather than waiting until a crisis happens, developing a set of signposts that enables early identification, planning, and execution can help better manage a brand's equity.

The proposed Brand Tragedy Index is one example of establishing a beacon for vulnerabilities on the road ahead. Leaders and key managers of organizations are encouraged to review these six signposts and modify or add to them according to one's brand and market situation. Similarly developing a BTI can help estimate current and potential brand risks and deploy this knowledge to build and rebuild brand relationships with customers and other stakeholders. Whether a brand tragedy arrives suddenly, or whether it festers over time, it is better to be prepared for it when it occurs than not.

Endnotes

1. Haig, Matt, *Brand Failures*. London: Kogan Page, 2003.
2. "When Corporate Innovation Goes Bad — The 160 Biggest Product Failures of All Time," *CBInsights Research Brief*, October 4, 2021. https://www.cbinsights.com/research/corporate-innovation-product-fails/ (Accessed May 28, 2022).
3. For more comprehensive treatments of leading teams and collaboration for results, see Hackman, J. Richard, *Leading Teams: Setting the Stage for Great Performance*. Cambridge, MA: Harvard Business School Publishing, 2002; and Hackman, J. Richard, *Collaborative Intelligence: Using Teams to Solve Hard Problems*. San Francisco: Berrett-Koehler Publishers, 2011.
4. Witzel, Morgen, *Tata: The Evolution of a Corporate Brand*. London: Penguin Books, 2010.
5. Tata.com website, https://www.tata.com/newsroom/titan-diversity-blazing-a-trail (Accessed May 25, 2022).
6. Sager, Fritz and Christian Rosser, "Historical Methods," in Mark Bevir und R.A.W. Rhodes (eds.). *The Routledge Handbook of Interpretive Political Science*. London/New York: Routledge, 2015.
7. For a discussion of brand architecture see: Keller, Kevin L. "Designing and Implementing Brand Architecture Strategies," *Journal of Brand Management*, 21, December 9, 2014, 702–715.
8. Reckendrees, Alfred, *Beiersdorf: The Company Behind the Brands NIVEA, tesa, Hansaplast and Co.*, Munich: C.H. Beck, 2018.
9. For an introduction and overview of data base management, see: Lemahieu, Wilfried, Seppe vanden Broucke, and Bart Baesens, *Principles of Database Management: The Practical Guide to Storing, Managing and Analyzing Big and Small Data*. New York: Cambridge University Press, 2018.
10. Holt, Douglas B., *How Brands Become Icons*. Boston: Harvard Business School Press, 2004.
11. Iglesias, Oriol, Nicholas Ind, and Majken Schultz, "History Matters: The Role of History in Corporate Brand Strategy," *Business Horizons*, 63, 1, pp. 51–60.
12. Linstone, Harold A. and Murray Turoff, *The Delphi Method: Techniques and Applications*. Reading, MA: Addison-Wesley, 1975.
13. Osborn, Adam F., *Applied Imagination: Principles and Procedures of Creative Thinking*, 2nd ed. New York: Scribners, 1957.

14. Gordon, William J., *Synectics*. New York: Harper and Row, 1961.
15. De Bono, Edward, *Lateral Thinking: Creativity Step by Step.* New York: Harper and Row, 1970.
16. Covey, Sean, Chris McChesney, and Jim Huling, *The 4 Disciplines of Execution: Achieving Your Wildly Important Goals.* New York: Simon and Schuster, 2012.
17. Gawande, Atul, *The Checklist Manifesto*. New York: Picador, 2009.
18. *Ibid.*, see Appendix, item number 4 (A checklist for checklists).

Index

well-framed response, 98
Wells, H. G., 98
Wikipedia, 20
Wind, Jerry, 5
Windows, 129
Witzel, Morgan, 147
Wolpert, Stanley, 6
word-of-mouth communication, 71

Wurtzel, Alan, 113, 122, 148
Wurtzel, Sam, 113–114

Y
YouTube, 59, 67, 72–73

Z
Zuckerberg, Mark, 105

Printed in the USA
CPSIA information can be obtained
at www.ICGtesting.com
JSHW011929241023
50596JS00001B/2

9 789811 268175